good friends
good food

Michael De Maria

First published in the USA 1996 by Sibling Press

Copyright © 1996 Sibling Press

Project Director: J.J. Smith-Moore

Editor: Nora Burba Trulsson

Design and Production: Sara R. Becker & J.J. Smith-Moore

Food Stylist and Assistant to Chef: Michael Hoobler

Text copyright © 1996 Nora Burba Trulsson

Recipes copyright © 1996 Michael DeMaria

Photographs copyright © 1996 David B. Moore

ISBN 0-9654265-0-5

Printed in Phoenix, Arizona

THE ROYAL PALMS

COOKBOOK

CHEF MICHAEL DeMARIA

TEXT NORA BURBA TRULSSON

PHOTOGRAPHY DAVID B. MOORE

SIBLING

PRESS

ARIZONA

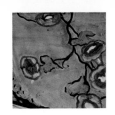

contents

our history

FOR DECADES, A RAMBLING WHITE WALL AND SPRAYS OF MAGENTA-COLORED BOUGAINVILLEA GENTLY GUARDED ONE OF PHOENIX'S BEST-KEPT SECRETS FROM THE HUSTLE AND BUSTLE OF DAILY CITY LIFE. BUT ONCE INSIDE THE WALLS OF THE ROYAL PALMS INN, VISITORS WERE HARD PRESSED TO LEAVE.

The Inn's old world charm, dramatic setting at the base of Camelback Mountain and its lush landscaping, perfumed by citrus blossoms and anchored by towering palms, proved mesmerizing to both locals and out-of-town visitors alike. For many of the Royal Palms' guests, there simply was no other place to stay.

Though the Royal Palms opened its doors to guests in 1948, the Inn's history dates back further. In fact, its development is linked to the development of agriculture and tourism in the Phoenix area.

In the late 1800s, the Anglo settlers of Phoenix dug out irrigation canals throughout the town, providing year 'round water and creating an agricultural mecca. They followed in the footsteps of the ancient Hohokam Indians, who, some 600 years earlier, had developed a sophisticated irrigation system to provide water for their crops. By the early 1900s, Phoenix was being touted in Eastern and Midwestern newspapers as a paradise for farmers, and there was a frenzy of experimentation with crops suitable for the hot desert climate. Citrus, it turned out, as well as dates, thrived in the central Arizona desert, particularly on the lower, southern slopes of Camelback Mountain. By the turn of the century, the area in which the Royal Palms is located was producing some of the first commercial crops of citrus (navel and Arizona Sweets oranges, and white marsh grapefruit) and dates in the state.

About the same time, the Southwest grew in its allure to tourists, thanks in part to the promotional

EFFORTS OF THE SANTA FE RAILROAD AND THE FRED HARVEY COMPANY. PHOENIX ALSO BENEFITED. VISITORS DISCOVERED ITS WARM, DRY WINTER CLIMATE, AND DOCTORS "PRESCRIBED" PROLONGED STAYS IN ARIZONA FOR PATIENTS WITH RESPIRATORY AILMENTS AND ARTHRITIS. SMALL INNS SPRANG UP AMIDST THE DESERT PATCHES AND CITRUS GROVES THAT EDGED THE BOTTOM OF CAMELBACK MOUNTAIN.

A SAVVY REAL ESTATE DEVELOPER COMBINED THE CONCEPTS OF AGRICULTURE AND HEALTHY LIVING IN 1919, CREATING ARCADIA, A NEW COMMUNITY SET IN THIS CITRUS-AND-DESERT LANDSCAPE NEAR THE MOUNTAIN ABOUT WHAT WAS THEN HALFWAY BETWEEN PHOENIX AND SCOTTSDALE.

ARCADIA WAS PLOTTED IN 5-, 20- AND 40-ACRE HOME SITES, AND ADVERTISEMENTS TOUTED THE CITRUS GROVES AND THE VIEWS OF CAMELBACK. A ROAD WAS PLANNED UP TO THE TOP OF THE MOUNTAIN, WHERE THE DEVELOPER PROMISED AN OASIS GARDEN AT THE SUMMIT.

THE ROAD AND THE ROSES AT THE TOP NEVER HAPPENED, AND IT TOOK THE COMMUNITY OF ARCADIA—WHICH EVENTUALLY BECAME PART OF PHOENIX—SEVERAL DECADES BEFORE IT REALLY DEVELOPED AT A PACE ENVISIONED BY ITS ORIGINATOR.

BY THE MID-1920s, A HANDFUL OF HARDY SOULS, PARTICULARLY THOSE BEST DESCRIBED AS "GENTLEMAN FARMERS," BEGAN BUILDING HOMES IN THE CITRUS GROVES. AMONG THOSE WAS DELOS WILLARD COOKE,

AN INDUSTRIALIST AND FINANCIER FROM NEW YORK, WHO BOUGHT 65 ACRES IN AN AREA OF ARCADIA CALLED CITRUS HOMES.

DELOS COOKE WAS BORN IN LEWISTON, NEW YORK IN 1863, SON OF A PRESBYTERIAN MINISTER, GRANDSON OF THE CONTROLLER OF NEW YORK STATE AND A MEMBER OF CONGRESS. COOKE'S FAMILY MOVED TO IOWA WHEN HE WAS YOUNG, AND IT WAS THERE THAT HE FIRST BEGAN WORKING FOR VARIOUS RAIL LINES. BY 1895, HE HAD JOINED THE ERIE RAILROAD, MOVED TO NEW YORK AND ROSE TO VICE PRESIDENT OF THE LINE.

DURING WORLD WAR I, COOKE WENT TO WASHINGTON, D.C. TO WORK ON TRANS-PORTATION FOR THE RED CROSS, AND SERVED ON A COMMITTEE OVERSEEING INLAND FREIGHT MOVEMENT WITHIN THE UNITED STATES. HE ALSO SERVED AS A FUEL ADMINISTRATOR IN NEW YORK CITY. AT THE WAR'S END, COOKE WAS HONORED FOR HIS CONTRIBUTIONS BY THE GOVERNMENTS OF FRANCE, ITALY AND GREAT BRITAIN. HE JOINED THE CUNARD STEAMSHIP LINE, WORKING FOR THE COMPANY BOTH IN THE UNITED STATES AND IN EUROPE. COOKE ALSO SERVED ON THE BOARD OF DIRECTORS FOR COMPANIES SUCH AS CHRYSLER MOTORS, THE BALTIMORE AND OHIO RAILROAD AND THE FOREMAN STATE BANK OF CHICAGO.

WITH HIS WIFE, FLORENCE, IN DELICATE HEALTH, AND THEIR ONLY SON,

Chauncey, on his own as a stockbroker in New York, Cooke opted for retirement in the mid-1920s—and a winter home in Phoenix, to escape the cold weather of the East Coast.

The Cookes asked Lescher & Mahoney, a long established Phoenix architectural firm, to draw up the plans for their "El Vernedero," or winter haven. Perhaps because it was a popular architectural style at the time—or possibly because of their many travels throughout southern Europe—the Cookes chose a Spanish Revival style for their home. White plaster over brick, Granada-tiled roofs, elaborate grillework for the windows and doorways, arches and stepped-back

masses marked the architecture of the house.

The "mansion" (at more than 3500 square feet, the original home was large by 1926 Phoenix standards) was sited at the end of a long driveway, flanked by towering palms. Visitors entered the Cooke home from the south, through a pair of huge wooden doors that opened onto a zaguan, or covered breezeway, which in turn opened onto the central courtyard. The home's floorplan was organized around this courtyard. To the east of the zaguan was the living room, marked by high, beamed ceilings and a dramatic fireplace; to the west was the guest bedroom. The Cookes' bedrooms and dressing areas occupied

LESCHER & MAHONEY
ARCHITECTS
PHOENIX — ARIZONA

A WINTER HOME FOR
MR. & MRS. DELOS W. COOKE
ARCADIA · PHOENIX · ARIZONA

ARCHITECTURAL

DATE · JUNE · 1926

THE REST OF THE WEST WING, AND THE NORTH WING COMPRISED THE DINING ROOM, KITCHEN AND BILLIARD ROOM. REFLECTING THE COOKES' GENTEEL LIFESTYLE, THERE WERE SMALLER ROOMS FOR SERVANTS, A CHAUFFEUR, STORAGE FOR TRAVEL TRUNKS AND A VAST LAUNDRY, PLUS A SEPARATE DINING ROOM FOR THE HELP, A TOOL ROOM, A GENEROUS GARAGE AND A SERVICE YARD, ALL OFF THE HOME'S NORTH WING.

IN KEEPING WITH A WARM-CLIMATE ARCHITECTURAL TRADITION, THE HOME HAD NO INTERIOR HALLWAYS EXCEPT FOR THOSE CONNECTING THE COOKES' BEDROOMS. TO GET FROM THE LIVING ROOM TO THE DINING ROOM, FOR EXAMPLE, THE COOKES, THEIR GUESTS AND THE HELP HAD TO TRAVEL THROUGH THE SHADED ARCADE, WHICH WAS LAID OUT ALONG THE PERIMETER OF THE COURTYARD. THE ARCADE WAS INTERSPERSED WITH ARCHWAYS THAT GAVE GLIMPSES OF THE LUSHLY PLANTED COURTYARD AND THE TILED, MOORISH-INFLUENCED REFLECTING POND.

THE COOKES WERE COLLECTORS OF ANTIQUES AND PLANTS. THEIR HOME WAS DECORATED WITH MANY EUROPEAN PIECES THOUGHT TO BE COLLECTED ON TRAVELS DURING THEIR YEARS ABROAD. IT WAS SAID THAT FLORENCE COOKE RECEIVED AN ANNUAL $10,000 ALLOWANCE FROM HER HUSBAND FOR THE GROUNDS, AND SHE FILLED THE GARDENS WITH RARE PALMS, SHRUBS, FLOWERS AND SPECIMEN CACTI.

IRONICALLY, THE COOKES WERE NOT TO SPEND MANY OF THEIR GOLDEN YEARS TOGETHER AT THEIR ARCADIA ESTATE. DELOS COOKE DIED OF CANCER IN A PHOENIX HOSPITAL IN 1931 AT THE AGE OF 67.

FLORENCE COOKE CONTINUED WINTERING AT THE HOME UNTIL 1937, WHEN SHE SOLD THE HOME TO W.E. TRAVIS, THEN THE PRESIDENT OF GREYHOUND BUS LINES, WHO

royal palms

ALSO USED IT AS A WINTER GETAWAY. TRAVIS
AND HIS WIFE ADDED A SECOND STORY TO THE
WEST WING OF THE HOUSE TO USE AS THEIR
PRIVATE QUARTERS. AT SOME POINT, A PRIEST,
A BAS-RELIEF SCULPTURE OF CHRIST AND AN
IN-HOME, SECOND-FLOOR CHAPEL BECAME
PART OF THE HOUSEHOLD
LANDSCAPE. WHEN HIS
WIFE DIED, W.E. TRAVIS
SOLD THE HOME TO JOHN
ROSS, PRESIDENT OF THE
AVIOLA RADIO COMPANY.

HOWEVER, ROSS
DIDN'T OWN THE HOME
FOR LONG. HE SOLD THE HOUSE AND ITS
30 ACRES OF CITRUS AND DATE PALMS TO A
GROUP OF INVESTORS HEADED BY FORMER
BAND LEADER AL STOVALL, WHO HAD MADE
HIS FORTUNE IN THE MANGANESE BUSINESS.
STOVALL AND HIS PARTNERS, ENVISIONING
A BOOM IN ARIZONA TOURISM AFTER WORLD

WAR II, BUILT 15 HOTEL ROOMS TO THE WEST
OF THE ORIGINAL COOKE HOME, AND CON-
VERTED THE MAIN HOME INTO MORE GUEST
ROOMS, A RECEPTION AREA AND DINING ROOM.
THE ROYAL PALMS INN OPENED TO GUESTS
IN THE WINTER OF 1948.

THE ROYAL PALMS
INN CHANGED HANDS SEV-
ERAL TIMES DURING THE
FIRST FEW YEARS OF OPER-
ATION. IN 1951, IT WAS SOLD
TO ANOTHER BUSINESSMAN
FOR $500,000, QUITE A
HANDSOME SUM FOR A
RESORT THEN OFFERING TENNIS, RIDING AND
SWIMMING TO ITS WINTER-SEASON GUESTS.
THERE WERE ALSO AN ADDITIONAL 45 CASITAS
BUILT WITHIN THE EASTERN GROVE OF CITRUS
TREES, AND A NEW HEART-SHAPED POOL, LINED
WITH ANTIQUE DELFT TILES, WAS SET BELOW
THE COOKE MANSION. LUCKILY, NONE OF

THE OWNERS DID MUCH TO CHANGE THE EXTERIOR OR INTERIOR OF THE ORIGINAL COOKE HOME.

THE ROYAL PALMS GAINED A CERTAIN CACHET WHEN CELEBRITY GUESTS BEGAN BOOKING WINTER VISITS THERE. HELENA RUBENSTEIN AND GROUCHO MARX WERE AMONG THOSE WHO RELAXED AMIDST THE PALMS AND THE FLOWERS. GUESTS CHECKED IN FOR THE ENTIRE SEASON—JANUARY THROUGH APRIL—AND DID SO FOR MANY DECADES.

ALONG THE WAY, A POPULAR PHOENIX LEGEND WAS BORN. SOMEHOW, THE "E" AT THE END OF THE COOKES' LAST NAME WAS DROPPED, AND DELOS COOKE EVOLVED INTO A MEMBER OF THE BRITISH THOMAS COOK TRAVEL FAMILY. IT WASN'T TRUE, BUT THE MYTH PREVAILED—PROBABLY BECAUSE THE EARLY HOTELIERS THOUGHT IT MADE GOOD COPY.

IN 1956, THE INN WAS AGAIN FOR SALE. THIS TIME IT WAS ACQUIRED BY CHARLES ALBERDING, A CHICAGO INVESTOR, AND HIS TEXAS-BASED ALSONETT HOTELS. AMONG ALSONETT'S MORE NOTABLE HOLDINGS WERE THE PEABODY HOTEL IN MEMPHIS AND THE TORREY PINES INN NEAR SAN DIEGO. ALBERDING, A SAVVY HOTELIER, HAD ALREADY ACQUIRED THE JOKAKE INN AND THE PARADISE INN, TWO POPULAR NEARBY RESORTS, ALSO AT THE BASE OF CAMELBACK MOUNTAIN. ROYAL PALMS WAS TO BE THE JEWEL OF HIS ARIZONA CROWN.

ALBERDING WENT TO WORK TRANS-FORMING THE ROYAL PALMS FROM A SLEEPY HIDEAWAY INTO AN ELEGANT COMPETITOR IN THE BURGEONING PHOENIX-AREA RESORT SCENE. A TIRELESS TRAVELER, ALBERDING FLEW TO PHOENIX AT LEAST TWICE A MONTH FROM CHICAGO TO OVERSEE ADDITIONS AND IMPROVEMENTS SUCH AS NEW MEETING ROOMS, THE EXPANSION OF THE DINING ROOM, A NEW

LOBBY AND RECEPTION AREA, A MODERN POOL AND THE ADDITION OF A TWO-STORY BUILDING, COMPLETE WITH UNDERGROUND PARKING AND HOTEL SUITES. ALBERDING'S RULE FOR HIS HOTELS WAS THAT THEY WERE TO BE FILLED WITH OIL PAINTINGS, CRYSTAL CHANDELIERS AND ORIENTAL RUGS. THE ROYAL PALMS HAD PLENTY OF ALL THREE.

AFTER A FIRE AT THE HOTEL IN THE EARLY 1970S, ALBERDING INSTALLED HIS LONG-TIME SECRETARY, PAT RYAN SAMFILIPPO OF CHICAGO, AS GENERAL MANAGER OF THE HOTEL. SHE WAS SUPPOSED TO SPEND A YEAR ORGANIZING THE HOTEL AND INSTEAD STAYED ON FOR 20. SAMFILIPPO PROVED TO BE A GRACIOUS INNKEEPER. HER DOGS (ONE, BARON, A GENTLE GERMAN SHEPHERD, WAS PARTICULARLY POPULAR WITH THE GUESTS) LOUNGED ON THE SOFAS IN THE LOBBY AND BECAME KNOWN AS THE FOUR-LEGGED DESK CLERKS.

UNDER SAMFILIPPO'S GUIDANCE, THE ROYAL PALMS BEGAN STAYING OPEN THROUGH THE SUMMERS IN THE LATE 1970S. IT WAS SHE WHO ALSO BEGAN BOOKING SMALL ORCHESTRAS AND SINGERS FOR THE INN'S ORANGE TREE DINING ROOM. THE ROYAL PALMS' ERA AS THE PLACE TO DANCE AND LISTEN TO

MUSICAL PERFORMERS IN PHOENIX BEGAN IN THE MID-1980S, WITH REGULAR APPEARANCES BY TONY MARTIN, FRANK SINATRA, JR., PATTY ANDREWS, SANDLER & YOUNG AND OTHERS, AS WELL AS THE HALLEMANS, POPULAR PHOENIX MUSICIANS. TABLES SKIRTED THE POLISHED DANCE FLOOR, COUPLES GLIDED IN GRACEFUL PRECISION—IT WAS AN ELEGANT WORLD WITHIN THE ENVELOPING WHITE WALLS OF THE ROYAL PALMS INN.

CHARLES ALBERDING DIED IN 1989 AT THE AGE OF 88. IT WAS THE END OF ONE ERA FOR THE ROYAL PALMS INN—AND THE BEGINNING OF A NEW ADVENTURE.

ALBERDING'S FAMILY SOLD THE PROPERTY TO JENNIFER AND FRED UNGER, LOCAL RESIDENTS, IN 1995. THE COUPLE HAD RECENTLY PUT THE FINISHING TOUCHES ON RESTORING ANOTHER HISTORIC HOTEL, THE HERMOSA INN IN NEARBY PARADISE VALLEY, WHICH WAS ONCE THE HOME AND STUDIO OF ARIZONA COWBOY ARTIST LON MEGARGEE.

AFTER A SPRING AND SUMMER OF RENOVATION AND RESTORATION OF THE ORIGINAL COOKE MANSION AND OTHER STRUCTURES ON THE ROYAL PALMS PROPERTY, THE UNGERS RE-OPENED THE HOTEL IN THE FALL OF 1996. THE BUILDING PROJECT LOOKED TO THE PAST FOR INSPIRATION AND BROUGHT THE PROPERTY BACK TO ITS 1930S CHARM, EMPHASIZING A SPANISH COLONIAL AMBIANCE IN THE BUILDINGS AND THE LUSHLY LANDSCAPED GROUNDS.

THE RESTAURANT AT THE ROYAL PALMS HAS BEEN RENAMED T. COOK'S, IN HONOR OF THE POPULAR LOCAL LEGEND, WITH CHEF MICHAEL DEMARIA AT THE HELM AND A MENU OF RUSTIC MEDITERRANEAN FARE TEMPTING NEWCOMERS AND ROYAL PALMS REGULARS ALIKE. NEWLY RENOVATED,

THE ROYAL PALMS CONTINUES TO DRAW VISITORS BECAUSE OF ITS OLD WORLD CHARM, THE PERFUME OF THE CITRUS BLOSSOMS, AND THE TOWERING PALMS, STILL STANDING SENTRY AT THE BASE OF MAJESTIC CAMELBACK MOUNTAIN.

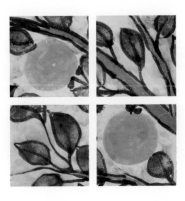

good morning

SIT DOWN AND FEED, WELCOME TO OUR TABLE.

~SHAKESPEARE

royal palms

BLUEBERRY CRUMBLE MUFFINS
Yields 6 Large Muffins

For the Crumb Topping: Blend butter, margarine and sugar with an electric mixer. Add flours, salt and vanilla extract, mixing until crumbly. *Yields 2 cups.*

For the Muffins: Preheat oven to 400°F. Cream butter and sugar with an electric mixer until light. Add eggs and beat with a spatula. Using the electric mixer, blend in flour, salt, vanilla extract, baking powder and sour cream until smooth. Fold in the blueberries with the spatula. Spray large muffin tins with vegetable oil baking spray. Fill muffin cups to the top edge. Sprinkle each muffin with about 2 tablespoons of the Crumb Topping. Bake at 400°F for 5 minutes, then reduce temperature to 375°F for about 15 minutes longer, or until muffin tops are no longer soft to touch.

For the Crumb Topping:
1/4 CUP BUTTER
1/4 CUP MARGARINE
1/3 CUP + 2 TABLESPOONS GRANULATED SUGAR
2/3 CUP ALL-PURPOSE FLOUR
2/3 CUP CAKE FLOUR
1/3 TEASPOON SALT
1 TEASPOON VANILLA EXTRACT

For the Muffins:
1/2 CUP BUTTER OR MARGARINE
1 CUP GRANULATED SUGAR
3 EGGS
2 CUPS ALL-PURPOSE FLOUR
1/4 TEASPOON SALT
1 TEASPOON VANILLA EXTRACT
1 TEASPOON BAKING POWDER
1/2 CUP SOUR CREAM
1 1/2 CUPS BLUEBERRIES, FRESH OR FROZEN
1 1/2 CUPS CRUMB TOPPING

BANANA-DATE BREAD

Yields 1 Large Loaf

1 1/2 CUPS PITTED DATES

2 CUPS HOT WATER

1 TABLESPOON BAKING SODA

3 RIPE BANANAS

3 CUPS GRANULATED SUGAR

5 EGGS

4 CUPS ALL-PURPOSE FLOUR

1 TEASPOON SALT

1 TEASPOON CLOVES, GROUND

1 TEASPOON GINGER, GROUND

1 TEASPOON NUTMEG, GROUND

1 1/2 TABLE-SPOONS COCOA POWDER

1/4 CUP MELTED BUTTER

1 1/2 CUPS WALNUTS, CHOPPED

Chef's note: Use this hearty bread for BANANA-DATE BREAD FRENCH TOAST WITH COUNTRY SAUSAGE. See page 26

Preheat oven to 325°F. Cover dates with hot water. Add baking soda, stirring to dissolve. With an electric mixer, beat together the bananas, sugar and eggs until they are light in color. Blend in dates with soda water. Add flour, salt, spices and cocoa powder. Blend in melted butter and nuts. Spray a large loaf pan with vegetable oil baking spray and fill 3/4 full with bread batter. Bake for about 70 minutes, or until a toothpick inserted into the center of the loaf comes out clean.

CARROT AND BRAN MUFFINS
Yields 6 to 8 Large Muffins

Preheat oven to 425°F. In a large mixing bowl, combine the bran, flour, brown sugar, salt, baking soda, raisins and carrots. In a separate bowl, mix together eggs, buttermilk, oil, molasses and honey. Blend pineapple into the liquids. Stir liquids into the dry mixture, stirring only enough to blend. Spray large muffin tins with vegetable oil baking spray. Fill muffin cups to top edge. Bake at 425°F for 5 minutes, then reduce oven temperature to 350°F. Bake for about 15 minutes longer, or until muffin tops are no longer soft to touch.

5 1/2 CUPS BRAN
4 CUPS WHOLE-WHEAT FLOUR
1/2 CUP BROWN SUGAR
1/2 TEASPOON SALT
2 TABLESPOONS BAKING SODA
2 1/2 CUPS RAISINS
1/3 CUP GRATED CARROTS
5 EGGS
4 CUPS BUTTERMILK
1/3 CUP VEGETABLE OIL
1/2 CUP MOLASSES
1 1/4 CUPS HONEY
1 CUP PINEAPPLE,
   CRUSHED

Chef's note: Preheating the oven is always important, particularly in baking. With this muffin recipe, the oven has to be hot enough for the dough to rise and stabilize before you lower the temperature. This ensures a desirably crispy muffin.

FRITTATA OF PANCETTA AND BALSAMIC ONIONS

Serves 1

For the Balsamic Onions: In a hot, non-stick skillet, sauté olive oil and onions for 5 to 7 minutes. Add balsamic vinegar and continue sautéing until nearly all is evaporated. Add sugar, salt and pepper, reducing to a syrupy consistency over high heat. Cool, then fold in parsley. *Yields 3/4 cup.*

For the Red Pepper Coulis: Using a blender, blend red pepper and Chicken Stock. Slowly add the olive oil. Strain. Add salt and pepper to taste. *Yields 3/4 cup.*

For the Frittata: Preheat the oven to 375°F. Using a blender, blend eggs and set aside. In a hot skillet, cook pancetta until crispy. Drain and reserve. Melt butter in a hot, oven-proof skillet. Add Balsamic Onions, garlic, tomatoes and cooked pancetta. Sauté for 3 to 4 minutes on medium-high heat. Pour in the eggs; add the cheese, basil, salt and pepper. Stir for 30 seconds until combined. Place the pan in the oven for 5 minutes, or until Frittata is spongy to the touch and lightly browned.

To Serve: Spoon 2 tablespoons Red Pepper Coulis onto an individual serving plate. Cut the Frittata into 4 wedges; arrange on plate. Garnish with the cantaloupe and mint.

For the Balsamic Onions:
2 TABLESPOONS OLIVE OIL
1 LARGE YELLOW ONION, PEELED AND SLICED INTO 1/8-INCH-THICK SLICES
1/4 CUP BALSAMIC VINEGAR
2 TABLESPOONS SUGAR
1/2 TEASPOON SALT
1/4 TEASPOON BLACK PEPPER
1 TABLESPOON PARSLEY, CHOPPED

For the Red Pepper Coulis:
1 RED BELL PEPPER, ROASTED, PEELED AND SEEDED
1/4 CUP CHICKEN STOCK*
1 TABLESPOON OLIVE OIL
SALT AND PEPPER TO TASTE

For the Frittata:
3 EXTRA-LARGE EGGS
1/4 CUP PANCETTA, CHOPPED
1 TABLESPOON BUTTER
1/4 CUP BALSAMIC ONIONS
1/2 TEASPOON GARLIC, MINCED
1/2 ROMA (ITALIAN PLUM) TOMATO, PEELED, SEEDED AND DICED
1/4 CUP FONTINA CHEESE, SHREDDED
1 TABLESPOON BASIL, SLICED INTO THIN STRIPS
1/2 TEASPOON SALT
1/4 TEASPOON BLACK PEPPER

For the Garnish:
2 TABLESPOONS RED PEPPER COULIS
2 WEDGES CANTALOUPE, PEELED AND SEEDED
1 SPRIG FRESH MINT

*See Appendix

BANANA-DATE BREAD FRENCH TOAST
WITH COUNTRY SAUSAGE
Serves 4

For the Country Sausage:
1 POUND BULK PORK SAUSAGE
1/2 POUND GROUND VEAL
1/4 POUND GROUND CHICKEN
1 BELL PEPPER, ROASTED, PEELED, SEEDED
　AND MINCED
4 LARGE ROAST SHALLOTS*, MINCED
1/4 CUP OLIVE OIL
1 TABLESPOON SAGE, CHOPPED
1 TABLESPOON BASIL, CHOPPED
1 TABLESPOON PARSLEY, CHOPPED
1 TABLESPOON ROAST GARLIC* PURÉE
1 TEASPOON FENNEL SEED, TOASTED
　AND CRUSHED
1/2 TABLESPOON RED CHILE FLAKES
1 TABLESPOON SALT
1 TEASPOON BLACK PEPPER

For the French Toast Batter:
6 EGGS
1/2 TEASPOON GROUND CINNAMON
1 TEASPOON VANILLA EXTRACT
1/4 CUP MILK
1 TEASPOON SUGAR

For Banana-Date Bread, See page 22

For the Sauce:
1/2 CUP BUTTER
1/2 CUP BROWN SUGAR
1 TABLESPOON VANILLA EXTRACT
1 TABLESPOON GRATED ORANGE RIND
1/2 CUP ORANGE JUICE
1/2 CUP MAPLE SYRUP

For the Garnish:
1 PINT (BASKET) RASPBERRIES

For the Country Sausage: In a mixing bowl, combine all ingredients, blending well. Form into 8 patties and grill until center is no longer pink. *Yields 8 patties.*

For the French Toast Batter: Mix together batter ingredients. Slice the cooled Banana-Date Bread into 1 1/4-inch-thick slices. Dip slices into batter, then place slices onto a well-greased, non-stick skillet, cooking until golden brown on both sides. Cut each slice into two triangle shapes and reserve.

For the Sauce: In a hot saucepan, heat butter and brown sugar for 1 minute. Add the vanilla, orange rind and juice, and maple syrup, cooking over medium-high heat for 6 more minutes. *Yields approximately 2 cups.*

To Serve: Arrange 4 triangles of the French Toast on each individual serving plate, then top with 1/2 cup Sauce. Finish with 2 Country Sausage patties on top of the toast. Garnish with about 12 raspberries per serving.

*See Appendix

EGGS MEDITERRANEAN
Serves 4

For the Tomato Hollandaise: In a metal mixing bowl, combine egg yolks with 1 tablespoon cold water. Place bowl over a saucepan of simmering water. Whisk yolks continuously until they become light and frothy, forming soft peaks. Keep sprinkling the remaining cold water around the inside rim of the metal bowl to prevent eggs from cooking or sticking to the bowl. Slowly whisk warm clarified butter and lemon juice into the yolks until all is incorporated. Add the tomato paste, cayenne, salt and pepper. Keep warm. *Yields 2 cups.*

For the Tuscan Olive Relish: Mix together vegetables, capers and garlic. Add olive oil, salt and pepper, tossing to coat. *Yields 1/2 cup.*

To Serve: Brush Focaccia Bread rounds with butter and griddle until warm. Poach eggs to medium. On each individual serving plate, top 2 Focaccia rounds with 1/4 pound of the sliced prosciutto. Top each round with a poached egg. Ladle 1/4 cup of Tomato Hollandaise over each poached egg and top each with 1 teaspoon of the Tuscan Olive Relish.

For the Tomato Hollandaise:
6 EGG YOLKS
3 TABLESPOONS COLD WATER
1 1/2 CUPS CLARIFIED BUTTER
2 TABLESPOONS LEMON JUICE
1 TABLESPOON TOMATO PASTE
1/4 TEASPOON CAYENNE PEPPER
1 TEASPOON SALT
1/2 TEASPOON BLACK PEPPER

For the Tuscan Olive Relish:
2 TABLESPOONS TOMATOES, PEELED, SEEDED AND DICED
2 TABLESPOONS KALAMATA OLIVES, PITTED AND FINELY DICED
2 TABLESPOONS GREEN OLIVES, PITTED AND FINELY DICED
2 TABLESPOONS RED PEPPERS, ROASTED, PEELED, SEEDED AND FINELY DICED
2 TABLESPOONS RED ONIONS, FINELY DICED
2 TEASPOONS CAPERS
1/2 TEASPOON GARLIC, FINELY DICED
2 TEASPOONS EXTRA-VIRGIN OLIVE OIL
1/4 TEASPOON SALT
1/4 TEASPOON BLACK PEPPER

To Serve:
8 2 1/2-INCH CIRCLES OF FOCACCIA BREAD*
BUTTER
8 EGGS
1 POUND PROSCIUTTO, THINLY SLICED

Chef's note: The secret to the hollandaise sauce in this recipe is warm~not hot~butter. Hot butter will cause the sauce to "break." To make clarified butter, melt the butter over medium-low heat. Remove it from heat and let the milk solids sink to the bottom. Skim off any fat that rises to the top and then ladle out the clear, melted butter.

*See Appendix

SMOKED SALMON ON POTATO PANCAKES WITH BOURSIN SAUCE

Serves 4

For the Smoked Salmon:

1 WHOLE SIDE SALMON, BONED
1/4 CUP SALT
1/4 CUP BROWN SUGAR
1/4 CUP GRANULATED SUGAR
2 TABLESPOONS FENNEL SEEDS, CRUSHED
2 TABLESPOONS OLIVE OIL
1/4 CUP FRESH DILL
1/4 CUP FRESH TARRAGON
1/4 CUP FRESH MINT
1 CUP ORANGE JUICE

For the Chive Salad:

1/2 CUP CHIVES, SLICED
    INTO 1-INCH
    PIECES
1/2 TEASPOON
    OLIVE OIL
1/4 TEASPOON
    BALSAMIC
    VINEGAR
PINCH OF PARSLEY
SALT AND PEPPER TO TASTE

For the Boursin Cheese Sauce:

1 TABLESPOON OLIVE OIL
2 TABLESPOONS SHALLOTS, CHOPPED
1/4 CUP CHARDONNAY
1 CUP HEAVY CREAM
1 CUP BOURSIN CHEESE

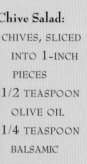

1/2 CUP CHICKEN STOCK*
1 TEASPOON SALT
1 TEASPOON BLACK PEPPER
2 TABLESPOONS CHIVES, CHOPPED
1 TABLESPOON PARSLEY, CHOPPED

For the Potato Pancakes:

2 SMALL RUSSET POTATOES,
    UNPEELED
1/2 YELLOW ONION, DICED
2 TEASPOONS SALT
1 TEASPOON PEPPER
2 TABLESPOONS PARSLEY,
    CHOPPED
1 TEASPOON GARLIC,
    MINCED
1 EGG
1 TABLESPOON MILK
1 TABLESPOON OLIVE OIL

For the Garnish:

1 BAGEL, SLICED INTO 4 THIN SLICES

*See Appendix

For the Smoked Salmon: Ask your butcher to prepare a side of salmon, completely boned. Combine salt, sugars and fennel seeds to make curing mixture. Place salmon on a sheet

Chef's note: This recipe requires a smoker for the salmon, but purchased smoked salmon can easily be substituted. To keep the potatoes in the Potato Pancake recipe from oxidizing, peel and shred them just before adding to the mixture.

pan. Rub salmon with the olive oil, then rub in half the curing mixture. Mix chopped herbs with orange juice, then pour over salmon. Sprinkle on remaining curing mixture. Cover salmon with plastic wrap and refrigerate for 3 days, basting once a day. When the salmon is cured, smoke it in a smoking oven between 60 and 80°F for 1 hour. Remove, wrap in plastic and refrigerate until use. *Yields 1 side salmon.*

For the Chive Salad: Toss all ingredients together. *Yields approximately 1/2 cup.*

For the Boursin Cheese Sauce: In a 2-quart saucepan, heat olive oil, add shallots and cook for 3 to 4 minutes on medium heat. Add wine and reduce until nearly evaporated. Stir in cream, cheese and chicken stock. Reduce by 1/4 volume until the sauce reaches a smooth consistency. Add salt, pepper, chives and parsley. Reserve warm. *Yields 2 cups.*

For the Potato Pancakes: Shred the potatoes with a medium hand-grater. In a mixing bowl, stir together potatoes with the remaining ingredients. Mix well. Spoon about 1/3-cup portions of the potato mixture onto a hot, oiled griddle to form 4 pancakes. Cook until golden brown on both sides. *Yields 4 pancakes.*

To Serve: Place a Potato Pancake onto the center of each individual serving plate. Top with thinly sliced Smoked Salmon. Sprinkle with Chive Salad, then spoon Boursin Cheese Sauce around the pancake. Garnish with a slice of bagel, which has been toasted and buttered.

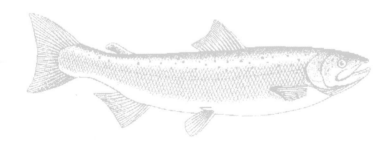

good afternoon

According to the Spanish proverb,

Four persons are wanted to make a good salad:

A Spendthrift for the oil, a Miser for the vinegar,

a Counselor for the salt and a Madman to stir it all up.

~Abraham Hayward

SMOKED ROMA TOMATO AND WHITE BEAN SOUP
Serves 4

For the Smoked Tomatoes: Heat the smoker to 170-200°F; add the soaked wood chips. Cut the tomatoes in half lengthwise, scoop out the pulp and discard or save for future use. Toss the scooped-out tomato halves with salt, pepper and olive oil. Place the tomatoes in the smoker and lightly smoke for 30 minutes. Remove and cool to room temperature. *Yields approximately 1 1/4 cups.*

For the White Beans: Simmer the pre-soaked white beans in Chicken Stock with the ham hock for 45 minutes to 1 hour, or until the beans are very tender. Drain, and spread the beans out to cool to room temperature. *Yields approximately 3 cups.*

For the Soup: Heat a saucepan on high, add olive oil and garlic, sautéing until golden. Add the Smoked Tomatoes and continue sautéing for 2 to 3 minutes. Add the White Beans and toss once or twice without breaking the beans. Add the Chicken Stock, salt and pepper, bringing to a rapid boil. Remove from heat and ladle into soup bowls. Sprinkle each bowl with basil and parsley; garnish with Parmesan.

For the Smoked Tomatoes:
1 CUP ALDER, PECAN, CHERRY OR MESQUITE CHIPS, SOAKED IN WATER FOR 12 HOURS
12 ROMA (ITALIAN PLUM) TOMATOES
1/2 TEASPOON SALT
1/2 TEASPOON BLACK PEPPER
2 TEASPOONS EXTRA-VIRGIN OLIVE OIL

For the White Beans:
1/2 POUND WHITE BEANS, SOAKED FOR 24 HOURS
1 QUART CHICKEN STOCK*
1 SMALL HAM HOCK

For the Soup:
2 TABLESPOONS OLIVE OIL
1/4 CUP GARLIC, SLICED
1 1/4 CUPS SMOKED TOMATOES
1 1/2 CUPS WHITE BEANS*
3 CUPS CHICKEN STOCK*
1 TEASPOON KOSHER SALT
1 TEASPOON BLACK PEPPER
2 TABLESPOONS BASIL, CHOPPED
1 TABLESPOON PARSLEY, CHOPPED
PARMESAN CHEESE, FINELY GRATED

*See Appendix

*Chef's note:
This is our version of a soup from the Barcelona area of Spain. You can use sun-dried tomatoes instead of smoked. You can also dry your own tomatoes in a 200°F oven. Just place the tomatoes pulp-side down on an oven rack with a baking pan underneath. Dry for approximately 3 1/2 hours.*

SAUTÉED MUSSELS IN
CHARDONNAY-THYME BROTH
Serves 1 or 2 as an appetizer

Heat a sauté pan, add the olive oil and heat 15 seconds more. Add shallots and mussels, and sauté. Add the Chardonnay, continue sautéing, and allow the wine to reduce by half. Add the clam juice, cream, garlic, herbs, salt and pepper. Cover the pan with a lid, allowing the mussels to steam for 2 to 3 minutes. When the mussels open, add butter and swirl until butter emulsifies into the broth. Discard any mussels that do not open after cooking.

To Serve: Place the toasted Italian bread in the bottom of a serving bowl, spoon the mussels over the bread, then pour on the broth.

2 TABLESPOONS OLIVE OIL
1 TEASPOON SHALLOTS, CHOPPED
1 POUND BLACK MUSSELS, WASHED
1/4 CUP CHARDONNAY
1/4 CUP CLAM JUICE
1 TABLESPOON HEAVY CREAM
1 TEASPOON GARLIC, CHOPPED
1 TEASPOON THYME, CHOPPED
1 TEASPOON PARSLEY, CHOPPED
PINCH SALT
PINCH BLACK PEPPER
1/4 CUP COLD BUTTER, CUT INTO PATS
1 THICK SLICE ITALIAN BREAD, TOASTED

*Chef's note:
To eat mussels
"Mediterranean
style," choose one
springy mussel shell,
remove the mussel
(eating it, of course!)
and use it as tongs
to eat the rest of
the mussels.*

BROILED SALMON NIÇOISE
Serves 4

For the Salmon: Coat the salmon fillets with the olive oil, season with salt and pepper, and sprinkle with tarragon. Grill to medium-rare.

For the Tarragon Vinaigrette: In a stainless steel mixing bowl, whisk together vinegar, garlic, shallots, mustard, herbs and seasonings. Let steep for 20 to 25 minutes. Slowly whisk in the olive oil. *Yields 3 cups.*

For the Niçoise Salad: Cut the potatoes into eighths and roast them in the oven. Cool and set aside. Trim green beans. Cook in boiling, salted water until desired tenderness, then plunge into cold water to stop the cooking process. In a mixing bowl, toss together the potatoes, beans, olives, lettuce, red onion and Tarragon Vinaigrette.

To Serve: Divide the Niçoise Salad among four individual serving plates. Top with the Salmon, dressed with a little bit of the Tarragon Vinaigrette. Garnish with the hard-boiled eggs.

For the Salmon:
4 4-OUNCE SALMON FILLETS
OLIVE OIL TO COAT THE SALMON
SALT AND PEPPER TO TASTE
1 TABLESPOON TARRAGON, CHOPPED

For the Tarragon Vinaigrette:
1/2 CUP TARRAGON VINEGAR
1 TABLESPOON GARLIC, CHOPPED
1 TABLESPOON SHALLOTS, CHOPPED
1 TABLESPOON WHOLE-GRAIN MUSTARD
2 TABLESPOONS TARRAGON, CHOPPED
1 TABLESPOON PARSLEY, CHOPPED
1 TABLESPOON CHIVES, CHOPPED
1 TEASPOON KOSHER SALT
1/2 TEASPOON BLACK PEPPER
1 TEASPOON SUGAR
1 1/2 CUPS OLIVE OIL

For the Niçoise Salad:
1 CUP NEW POTATOES
1 CUP FRENCH GREEN BEANS
1/2 CUP WHOLE KALAMATA OLIVES
4 CUPS BABY GREENS (FRISÉE, RED OAK, SPINACH)
1 TABLESPOON CAPERS
1/4 CUP RED ONION, CHOPPED
TARRAGON VINAIGRETTE TO COAT THE SALAD

FOR THE GARNISH:
4 HARD-BOILED EGGS, COOLED AND CUT INTO QUARTERS

Chef's note: For the Tarragon Vinaigrette, steeping the herbs and seasonings for 20 to 25 minutes allows the vinegar to extract the flavors from the ingredients before the oil locks them in.

ROMAINE AND ARTICHOKE SALAD

Serves 4

For the Garlic Vinaigrette:

2 TABLESPOONS GARLIC, CHOPPED

1/2 CUP RED WINE VINEGAR

1 TABLESPOON ANCHOVY PASTE

1 TABLESPOON DIJON MUSTARD

1/4 CUP PARMESAN CHEESE, FINELY GRATED

2 TABLESPOONS PARSLEY, CHOPPED

1 TEASPOON SALT

1 TEASPOON BLACK PEPPER

1 1/2 CUPS OLIVE OIL

For the Salad:

2 HEADS OF ROMAINE LETTUCE, WASHED, DRIED AND SEPARATED INTO LEAVES

1 CAN ARTICHOKE BOTTOMS, SLICED THIN

2 TOMATOES, DICED

1/4 CUP GARLIC VINAIGRETTE

1 TABLESPOON BASIL, CHOPPED

1 TABLESPOON CAPERS

Chef's note: We use the "hearts," or the inner leaves of romaine for this salad. Save the outer leaves to make a spinach-like side dish. Simply chop the romaine leaves and sauté them in a bit of olive oil. Season to taste.

For the Garlic Vinaigrette: Mix garlic, vinegar, anchovy paste, Dijon mustard, Parmesan cheese and parsley together in a mixing bowl. Season with salt and pepper. Whisk in olive oil; adjust seasonings to taste. *Yields approximately 2 1/4 cups.*

For the Salad: Toss romaine, artichokes and tomatoes with the Garlic Vinaigrette. On individual serving plates, place dressed romaine leaves atop one another, making sure the artichokes and tomatoes are also evenly distributed. Sprinkle with basil and capers.

GRILLED VEGETABLE PRIMAVERA
WITH ORECCHIETTE

Serves 4

For the Grilled Vegetables: Lightly oil and season the vegetables. Grill until they begin to caramelize and become slightly transparent.

For the Primavera with Orecchiette: In a hot saucepan, sauté the Grilled Vegetables in the olive oil for about 2 to 3 minutes. Add the Chicken and Mushroom stocks and cook for 2 more minutes. Add the cooked pasta, mixing well. Add the butter and mix. Add the parsley, salt and pepper. Sprinkle with Parmesan cheese to taste.

For the Grilled Vegetables:
1 ZUCCHINI, SLICED LENGTHWISE INTO 1/4-INCH-THICK SLICES
1 BUNCH BROCCOLI, SLICED LENGTHWISE INTO 1/4-INCH-THICK SLICES
1/4 EGGPLANT, PEELED AND SLICED INTO 1/4-INCH-THICK SLICES
1 RED ONION, SLICED INTO 1/2-INCH-THICK SLICES
2 RED BELL PEPPERS, CUT INTO 4 SIDES
OLIVE OIL FOR GRILLING
SALT AND PEPPER TO TASTE
1 TABLESPOON PARSLEY, CHOPPED

For the Primavera with Orecchiette:
GRILLED VEGETABLES
1/4 CUP OLIVE OIL
1/4 CUP CHICKEN STOCK*
1/4 CUP MUSHROOM STOCK*
1 POUND ORECCHIETTE PASTA, COOKED AL DENTE
1/4 CUP COLD BUTTER, CUT INTO PATTIES
1 TEASPOON PARSLEY, CHOPPED
1 TEASPOON SALT
1 TEASPOON BLACK PEPPER
GRATED PARMESAN CHEESE

*See Appendix

Chef's note: Orecchiette is pasta shaped like little ears. It is usually available in Italian groceries or specialty food shops. An eggless pasta, orecchiette is great for vegan vegetarians.

GRILLED VEGETABLE SANDWICH WITH PESTO

Serves 4

For the Pesto:

1 CUP BASIL LEAVES

1/4 CUP PARMESAN CHEESE, FINELY GRATED

1/4 CUP PINE NUTS, TOASTED

1/4 CUP OLIVE OIL

1/2 TEASPOON SALT

1/4 TEASPOON BLACK
   PEPPER

1/8 CUP FETA CHEESE,
   FINELY GRATED

**For the Grilled
Vegetable Sandwich:**

1/2 EGGPLANT, SLICED 1/4-
   INCH THICK

2 LARGE RED BELL
   PEPPERS,
   QUARTERED AND
   SEEDED

1 LARGE ZUCCHINI,
   SLICED 1/4-INCH THICK

2 BEEFSTEAK TOMATOES, SLICED 1/4-
   INCH THICK

OLIVE OIL TO COAT THE VEGETABLES

1 TABLESPOON SALT

1 TABLESPOON BLACK PEPPER

4 4x4-INCH SQUARES OF FOCACCIA
   BREAD*

4 TABLESPOONS PESTO

*See Appendix

Chef's note:
Use your favorite purchased focaccia bread if you don't have the time to bake. You can also use this Pesto for dressings; as the basis of a marinade for fish, chicken or beef; or spread it on crostini as an appetizer.

For the Pesto: Remove stems from the basil leaves and pack tightly to make 1 cup. In a food processor, add basil, Parmesan cheese and pine nuts; purée. Add olive oil slowly until all is incorporated. Season with salt and pepper, then fold in feta cheese.

Yields 3/4 cup.

For the Grilled Vegetable Sandwich: Peel the eggplant slices, salt and let stand for six hours. When the eggplant is drained, oil and season all vegetables. Grill over a wood fire until warmed. Cut the Focaccia Bread and grill until warm. Remove the bread from the grill and spread each piece with 1 tablespoon Pesto. Layer vegetables atop the bread, then cut into wedges for serving. Serve with either fresh fruit or Pommes Frites*.

ROAST CHICKEN SALAD
Serves 2

On each individual serving plate, fan 1 tomato and 1/2 cucumber around the plate. Slice lengthwise and fan 1 Roast Chicken breast at the top and bottom of each plate. Shred the thigh meat from the Roast Chicken and toss with the endive, red oak, spinach and 2 tablespoons of the Balsamic Vinaigrette. Season with salt and pepper to taste. Drizzle the tomatoes and cucumbers on both plates with the rest of the vinaigrette. Place half of the greens mixture on each plate, top with feta cheese and chives, and season to taste.

2 TOMATOES, THINLY SLICED
1 MEDIUM CUCUMBER, THINLY SLICED
2 BREASTS FROM A ROAST CHICKEN*
2 THIGHS FROM A ROAST CHICKEN*, SKINNED
2 SMALL BELGIAN ENDIVES, JULIENNED
1 CUP BABY RED OAK LEAVES, JULIENNED
1 CUP BABY SPINACH, JULIENNED
3 TABLESPOONS BALSAMIC VINAIGRETTE*
2 TABLESPOONS FETA CHEESE, CRUMBLED
1 TEASPOON CHIVES, CHOPPED
SALT AND PEPPER TO TASTE

*See Appendix

Chef's note:
This is one of our most popular luncheon salads. Discarding the chopped lemons, you can use the rest of the Roast Chicken to make Chicken Stock

GRILLED GARLIC CHICKEN ON MUSHROOM RISOTTO
Serves 4

For the Mushroom Risotto: Re-hydrate the dried porcini mushrooms for 24 hours in enough water to cover. Drain, reserving the liquid, and chop the mushrooms. Heat olive oil in a 2-quart saucepan for 1 minute, then add shallots and button and porcini mushrooms. Sauté over medium heat for 5 minutes. Add the Chardonnay and cook until almost reduced. Add the rice and sauté for 1 minute. Add the mushroom water and cook until the water is absorbed. Add a little hot Chicken Stock at a time, until all is added. Add cream and reduce to a thick, creamy consistency. Add butter and season with salt and pepper. Just before serving, add Parmesan and herbs. *Yields approximately 4 1-cup servings.*

For the Grilled Garlic Chicken: Rub the chicken breasts with the Roast Garlic purée and the olive oil, and season with the salt, pepper and half of the rosemary and parsley. Grill over a wood or charcoal fire until tender and juicy, approximately 20 minutes. Sprinkle with the remaining herbs.

To Serve: Divide the Mushroom Risotto into 4 portions. On an individual serving plate, center a portion of Mushroom Risotto, then top with a Grilled Garlic Chicken breast. Toss the greens with the Chianti Vinaigrette, then place a small handful of the dressed salad on top of the chicken, with some spilling onto the plate. Drizzle more Chianti Vinaigrette around the plate and sprinkle with a pinch each of chopped rosemary and parsley for garnish.

For the Mushroom Risotto:
1 CUP DRIED PORCINI MUSHROOMS
WATER
2 TABLESPOONS OLIVE OIL
1/4 CUP SHALLOTS, CHOPPED
1 CUP WHITE BUTTON MUSHROOMS, SLICED
1/4 CUP CHARDONNAY
2 CUPS ARBORIO RICE
1/2 CUP WATER FROM REHYDRATED PORCINIS
6 CUPS CHICKEN STOCK*, HOT
1/2 CUP HEAVY CREAM
1/4 POUND BUTTER
1 TABLESPOON SALT
1 TEASPOON BLACK PEPPER
1/4 CUP PARMESAN CHEESE, FINELY GRATED
1 TABLESPOON PARSLEY, CHOPPED
1 TABLESPOON SAGE, CHOPPED

For the Grilled Garlic Chicken:
4 CHICKEN BREASTS, FIRST WING BONE ATTACHED
1/4 CUP ROAST GARLIC* PURÉE
PINCH SALT
1 TABLESPOON OLIVE OIL
PINCH BLACK PEPPER
1 TEASPOON ROSEMARY, CHOPPED
1 TEASPOON PARSLEY, CHOPPED

For the Greens:
2 CUPS BABY GREENS
1/4 CUP CHIANTI VINAIGRETTE*

*See Appendix

Chef's note: The trick to a good risotto is the cooking of the rice by adding hot liquid a little at a time until it reaches the desired thick, creamy consistency.

good evening

THE DISCOVERY OF A NEW DISH DOES MORE FOR

HUMAN HAPPINESS THAN THE DISCOVERY OF A STAR.

~BRILLAT-SAVARIN

MEDITERRANEAN APPETIZER PLATTER
Serves 4

For the Crostini:

4 DIAGONAL SLICES FRENCH BREAD, FROM
    A BAGUETTE

OLIVE OIL

2 TABLESPOONS BOURSIN CHEESE

1 TABLESPOON HEAVY CREAM

1 TABLESPOON ZUCCHINI,
    FINELY DICED

1 TABLESPOON CARROT,
    FINELY DICED

2 TEASPOONS EXTRA-VIRGIN
    OLIVE OIL

1 TABLESPOON YELLOW
    SQUASH, FINELY DICED

PINCH SALT

PINCH PEPPER

4 LARGE BASIL LEAVES, CUT
    INTO FINE STRIPS

**For the Vegetables and
Other Appetizers:**

1 CUP BABY GREENS
    (FRISÉE, RED OAK, SPINACH)

2 LARGE GRILLED MUSHROOMS*

1/4 CUP BALSAMIC VINAIGRETTE*

2 RED BELL PEPPERS, ROASTED, PEELED AND SEEDED

1/2 CUP KALAMATA OLIVES

1 BUNCH ASPARAGUS SPEARS, BLANCHED
    AND CUT TO 4-INCH LENGTHS

2 ROMA (ITALIAN PLUM) TOMATOES, SLICED THICK

8 THIN SLICES PROSCIUTTO

1 (8-OUNCE) BUFFALO MOZZARELLA,
    SLICED THICK

1 TABLESPOON EXTRA-VIRGIN OLIVE OIL

SALT AND PEPPER TO TASTE

For the Garnish:

6 BASIL TOPS

For the Crostini: Preheat oven to 400°F. Brush the bread slices with olive oil. Bake the bread for 10 minutes, or until crisp and golden brown. Remove from oven. Mix together the Boursin cheese and the cream. Spread on the Crostini. Toss the vegetables together with the olive oil, salt and pepper. Place equal amounts on each Crostini. Top each with the basil strips.

For the Vegetables and Other Appetizers: Dress the baby greens and Grilled Mushrooms with the Balsamic Vinaigrette. Sprinkle the peppers, olives, asparagus, tomatoes, prosciutto and mozzarella with the olive oil; add salt and pepper to taste.

To Serve: On a large platter, arrange Crostinis, greens, mushrooms, vegetables, olives, prosciutto and mozzarella. Garnish with basil tops.

*See Appendix

FIRE-ROASTED VEGETABLE-TURKEY SOUP

Serves 4

For the Fire-Roasted Vegetables: Peel and slice the eggplant and carrot lengthwise. Slice the zucchini lengthwise, and slice the red onion. Slice the red bell peppers lengthwise into quarters. Brush the vegetables with oil; season with salt and pepper. Grill the vegetables over a wood or charcoal fire until they soften somewhat and the peppers blacken. Remove the vegetables. Place the peppers in a bowl covered with plastic wrap so that the peppers will "sweat" and the peel can easily be removed. Cube all vegetables. *Yields 3 cups.*

For the Soup: Heat the olive oil in a large, hot saucepan. Add the garlic and sauté until golden brown. Add the cubed Fire-Roasted Vegetables and sauté for 2 more minutes. Add the Chicken Stock and boil for 1 minute. Add the tagliatelle pasta and the turkey; season to taste. Before serving, garnish with parsley and oregano.

For the Fire-Roasted Vegetables:
1/2 SMALL EGGPLANT
1 LARGE CARROT
1 SMALL ZUCCHINI
1 RED ONION
2 RED BELL PEPPERS
OLIVE OIL TO COAT VEGETABLES
SALT AND PEPPER TO TASTE

For the Soup:
2 TABLESPOONS OLIVE OIL
2 TEASPOONS GARLIC, SLICED
3 CUPS FIRE-ROASTED VEGETABLES
1 QUART CHICKEN STOCK*
1 CUP TAGLIATELLE PASTA, COOKED AND DRAINED
1 CUP ROASTED TURKEY MEAT, SHREDDED INTO STRIPS
SALT AND PEPPER TO TASTE

FOR THE GARNISH:
1 TABLESPOON PARSLEY, CHOPPED
1 TABLESPOON OREGANO, CHOPPED

*See Appendix

Chef's note: Be it Thanksgiving or any time of year, this is a great recipe for leftover roast turkey.

APPLE-ARUGULA SALAD WITH GORGONZOLA
Serves 4

4 OUNCES ARUGULA

4 HEADS OF ENDIVE, SLICED ON THE BIAS

3 TABLESPOONS GORGONZOLA CHEESE, CRUMBLED

1 RED APPLE, JULIENNED

5 TABLESPOONS CHIANTI VINAIGRETTE*

1 TEASPOON PARSLEY, CHOPPED

1 TEASPOON CHIVES, CHOPPED

Chef's note: To prevent oxidation, slice the endive and the apple just before serving.

In a stainless steel mixing bowl, lightly toss together the arugula, endive, 2 tablespoons of the Gorgonzola and the julienned apple. Drizzle in 4 tablespoons of the Chianti Vinaigrette; toss until well coated. Divide salad among four individual serving plates, centering the salad. Sprinkle with herbs. Use the remaining Chianti Vinaigrette and Gorgonzola to garnish the plates.

*See Appendix

ANGEL HAIR PASTA WITH GRILLED PORTOBELLO MUSHROOMS

Serves 4

In a hot sauté pan, add olive oil, garlic and shallots, sautéing until browned. Add the Grilled Mushrooms and peppers, sautéing for 1 more minute. Add the Chicken Stock, cooking for 4 to 5 minutes. Add the Mushroom Stock, salt and pepper to taste and continue cooking for an additional 2 minutes. Add the hot pasta, butter and spinach; toss well. Garnish with parsley.

2 TABLESPOONS OLIVE OIL
2 TABLESPOONS GARLIC, SLICED
1 TABLESPOON SHALLOTS, CHOPPED
4 GRILLED MUSHROOMS*, SLICED INTO STRIPS
2 RED BELL PEPPERS, ROASTED, PEELED,
   SEEDED AND JULIENNED
1/2 CUP CHICKEN STOCK*
1/2 CUP MUSHROOM STOCK*
SALT AND PEPPER TO TASTE
24 OUNCES ANGEL HAIR PASTA,
   COOKED AL DENTE
2 TABLESPOONS BUTTER
2 CUPS FRESH SPINACH, CUT
   INTO STRIPS

FOR THE GARNISH:
2 TABLESPOONS PARSLEY

*Chef's note:
The butter in this recipe emulsifies the sauce for a richer flavor. It can be left out.*

*See Appendix

PAELLA
Serves 4

For the Saffron Rice:

2 TABLESPOONS OLIVE OIL

1/2 CUP ONIONS, CHOPPED

PINCH SAFFRON THREADS

1/2 CUP CHARDONNAY

1 1/2 CUPS LONG-GRAIN WHITE RICE

2 1/2 CUPS CHICKEN STOCK*

1 TEASPOON SALT

1/2 TEASPOON BLACK PEPPER

2 TABLESPOONS PARSLEY, CHOPPED

For the Paella:

2 TABLESPOONS OLIVE OIL

1/4 CUP RED BELL PEPPERS, COARSELY DICED

1/4 CUP ONION, COARSELY DICED

1 TABLESPOON GARLIC, CHOPPED

1/2 CUP ANDOUILLE SAUSAGE, DICED

1 TABLESPOON THYME, CHOPPED

1/2 POUND CLAMS OR SMALL COCKLES

1/2 POUND BLACK MUSSELS

1/2 POUND SHRIMP, PEELED AND CLEANED

1/2 POUND COOKED CHICKEN MEAT, SHREDDED

3/4 CUP CLAM JUICE

2 CUPS SAFFRON RICE

2 TABLESPOONS PARSLEY, CHOPPED

1 TEASPOON BASIL, CHOPPED

1 TEASPOON ROSEMARY, CHOPPED

SALT AND PEPPER TO TASTE.

*See Appendix

For the Saffron Rice: Preheat oven to 350° F. In a saucepan, heat olive oil and sauté onions until they begin to sweat, about 4 minutes. Add the saffron threads and wine, reducing by 1/2 volume. Add the rice and sauté for 3 minutes. Add the Chicken Stock, salt and pepper, mix well and transfer rice mixture to an oven-proof dish with a tight-fitting lid. Place in oven and cook for 20 minutes, or until rice is tender. Cool to room temperature and sprinkle with parsley. *Yields 2 cups.*

For the Paella: Heat a large saucepan. Add olive oil, peppers, onions, garlic, sausage and half the thyme, sautéing for 3 to 5 minutes. Add clams (or cockles) and mussels, cover and cook until the first shellfish begin to open. Add the shrimp and cover again, cooking for 1 minute. Add the chicken, stir and then add the clam juice. Cover and cook for 1 minute. Add cooked Saffron Rice, cover again and cook for 2 more minutes. Remove cover and sprinkle with herbs, including remaining thyme. Season to taste. Fluff the Paella and serve in a large bowl.

LINGUINE WITH ROCK SHRIMP

Serves 4

For the Garlic Confit:
3/4 CUP GARLIC CLOVES, PEELED
1 CUP OLIVE OIL

For the Linguine and Shrimp:
3 TABLESPOONS OLIVE OIL
2 TABLESPOONS SHALLOTS,
  CHOPPED
1/2 CUP GARLIC CONFIT
1 CUP SUN- OR OVEN-
  DRIED TOMATOES
1 1/4 POUNDS ROCK
  SHRIMP
1/2 CUP CLAM JUICE
1/2 CUP SHRIMP STOCK*
2 TABLESPOONS HEAVY
  CREAM
24 OUNCES LINGUINE,
  COOKED AL DENTE
2 TABLESPOONS COLD
  BUTTER
SALT AND PEPPER TO TASTE

FOR THE GARNISH:
1 TABLESPOON PARSLEY, CHOPPED
1 TABLESPOON OREGANO, CHOPPED

*See Appendix

For the Garlic Confit: In a hot sauté pan, sauté garlic with 1/4 of the olive oil until golden. Add remainder of oil, simmering until garlic is soft with caramelized spots. Transfer garlic and oil to a bowl; cool. Refrigerate. To use, drain oil.

Yields 1/2 cup.

For the Linguine and Shrimp: Heat oil in a hot sauté pan. Sauté shallots, Garlic Confit and tomatoes in the oil for 2 minutes. Add shrimp and sauté for about 2 more minutes. Add clam juice, Shrimp Stock and cream, reducing to 1/4 volume. Add hot linguine and butter to the sauce, tossing until butter is incorporated. Season with salt and pepper. Serve in individual pasta bowls, garnishing with the herbs.

RIGATONI POMODORO

Serves 4

In a hot sauté pan, cook the olive oil, tomatoes, shallots and garlic over high heat for 3 minutes, reducing some of the excess liquid. Add the Chicken Stock and reduce to 1/4 volume. Add half the herbs and all the salt and pepper. Add hot pasta and butter to the tomato sauce; toss well. Serve in individual bowls, sprinkled with remaining herbs and Romano cheese.

3/4 CUP EXTRA-VIRGIN OLIVE OIL

8 ROMA (ITALIAN PLUM) TOMATOES, PEELED, SEEDED AND DICED

1 TABLESPOON SHALLOTS, CHOPPED

2 TABLESPOONS GARLIC, SLICED THIN

1 CUP CHICKEN STOCK*

2 TABLESPOONS PARSLEY, CHOPPED

2 TABLESPOONS BASIL, CHOPPED

1 TEASPOON SALT

1/2 TEASPOON BLACK PEPPER

1 TABLESPOON BUTTER

1 POUND RIGATONI, COOKED AL DENTE

SHAVED ROMANO CHEESE

*See Appendix

Chef's note: You can add extra vegetables to this dish to create a primavera-style pasta, or add prepared shrimp, fish or chicken to make this a heartier dish.

ROAST CHICKEN
WITH HERB MASHED POTATOES
Serves 2

For the Chicken:
31/2 POUND ROAST CHICKEN*
1/4 CUP ROAST CHICKEN* PAN DRIPPINGS

For the Herb Mashed Potatoes:
12 RED-SKINNED POTATOES, UNPEELED
1 TABLESPOON ROAST GARLIC* PURÉE
1/4 CUP HEAVY CREAM
1/4 CUP COLD BUTTER, CUBED
1 TEASPOON CHIVES, CHOPPED
1 TEASPOON PARSLEY, CHOPPED
1/2 TEASPOON OREGANO, CHOPPED
1 TEASPOON SALT
1/2 TEASPOON BLACK PEPPER

For the Corn and Mushroom Relish:
1 EAR WHITE CORN, UNHUSKED
1 CUP CHICKEN STOCK*
1/2 CUP MILK
1/2 CUP BUTTER
1 TABLESPOON SUGAR
1 TEASPOON SALT
1/2 TEASPOON BLACK PEPPER
8 LARGE MUSHROOMS, SLICED
1 TEASPOON BUTTER
SALT AND PEPPER TO TASTE
1 TABLESPOON PARSLEY, CHOPPED

*See Appendix

For the Chicken: Carve chicken into two breasts and two leg/thigh sections. Warm pan drippings and reserve.

For the Potatoes: Boil unpeeled potatoes until tender. Drain, keeping warm, and place in a mixing bowl. Add the Roast Garlic purée, cream and butter. Hand-mash until all ingredients are incorporated, but the mixture is still chunky. Add the herbs and seasonings, mixing carefully. *Yields 3 cups.*

For the Relish: Cut the ends off the ear of corn. Bring the Chicken Stock, milk, 1/2 butter, sugar, salt and pepper to a slow boil. Cook the corn in the milk mixture for 15 minutes or until tender. Shuck the corn. Cut the kernels off the cob. Sauté the mushrooms in the remaining butter until tender, then chop finely. Mix corn, mushrooms, salt, pepper and parsley. *Yields approximately 1 cup.*

To Serve: For each serving, spoon about 1 cup of the Potatoes onto the center of the plate. Lean a Roast Chicken breast and leg section against the Potatoes. Spoon on about 1/4 cup of the Relish and drizzle with the pan drippings.

Good 2/01 did Friday Sally & Doug

TUSCAN BEEF TENDERLOIN
WITH ROAST SHALLOTS

Serves 4

For the Tuscan Beef Rub:

1/4 CUP ROAST GARLIC* PURÉE

1 SMALL ONION, ROASTED SOFT AND PURÉED

1/4 TEASPOON CAYENNE PEPPER

1/4 TEASPOON BLACK PEPPER

1/4 CUP OLIVE OIL

1 TABLESPOON OREGANO, CHOPPED

For the Beef:

2 POUNDS BEEF TENDERLOIN, TRIMMED

TO SERVE:

1 1/3 CUPS BEEF DEMI-GLACE*

16 ROAST SHALLOTS*

POMMES FRITES*

*See Appendix

Chef's note: *There's no salt in the Tuscan Beef Rub mixture as salt will drain the juice from the beef. We add salt just before grilling.*

For the Tuscan Beef Rub: Mix together all ingredients. *Yields approximately 1/2 cup.*

For the Beef: Coat the meat with the Tuscan Beef Rub. Grill until rare or medium-rare, then slice into medallions.

To Serve: Ladle about 1/3 cup Beef Demi-Glace onto each serving plate, then arrange 4 2-ounce slices of Beef on each plate. Serve 4 Roast Shallots per plate, and the Pommes Frites.

SAGE-PISTACHIO LAMB WITH BEAN MASH AND BRAISED VEGETABLES

Serves 4

For the Bean Mash:
1/4 CUP OLIVE OIL
1 HAM HOCK
2 GARLIC CLOVES, SLICED
1 POUND DRIED GREAT NORTHERN BEANS,
    SOAKED FOR 24 HOURS
1 BAY LEAF
1 QUART CHICKEN STOCK*
1/2 CUP HEAVY CREAM
1 TEASPOON CHIVES, CHOPPED
1 TEASPOON PARSLEY, CHOPPED
2 TEASPOONS SALT
1 TEASPOON BLACK PEPPER
1/2 CUP BUTTER, CUBED
1 TABLESPOON SHERRY VINEGAR

For the Braised Vegetables:
1/4 CUP OLIVE OIL
3 CARROTS, CUT INTO CHUNKS
4 ONIONS, CUT INTO WEDGES WITH ROOT
    ATTACHED
3 RUTABAGAS, PEELED AND CUT INTO CHUNKS
3 TURNIPS, PEELED AND CUT INTO CHUNKS
1 TABLESPOON SHALLOTS, SLICED
1 QUART LAMB DEMI-GLACE*
1 TEASPOON PARSLEY, CHOPPED

For the Sage-Pistachio Pesto:
1/2 CUP UNSALTED PISTACHIO NUTS

1 CUP SAGE LEAVES
1/2 CUP OLIVE OIL
1 TEASPOON BLACK PEPPER

For the Lamb:
1 1/2 POUNDS LEG OF LAMB
1/2 CUP SAGE-PISTACHIO PESTO

For the Garnish:
1 CUP LAMB DEMI-GLACE*
1 TABLESPOON SAGE, CHOPPED

*See Appendix

For the Bean Mash: Heat a large stock pot. Add olive oil, ham hock and garlic, sautéing for 3 to 5 minutes. Add the drained and rinsed beans, bay leaf and Chicken Stock and simmer for approximately 2 hours, or until beans are soft. Drain, reserving beans and ham hock. Dice ham into small pieces; reserve. In a saucepan, hand-mash beans and cook over low heat until dry, about 10 to 15 minutes. Add cream, diced ham hock, herbs, salt and pepper. Stir in butter until incorporated. Add sherry vinegar, mixing well.

Yields approximately 1 1/2 cups.

For the Braised Vegetables: Preheat oven to 375°F. Heat an oven-proof saucepan on the cooktop. Add olive oil, vegetables and shallots, sautéing for 4 to 5 minutes. Cover the vegetables with the Lamb Demi-Glace, cover the pan and place in the oven for 45 minutes to 1 hour, or until the vegetables are tender. Sprinkle with parsley.

Yields 4 servings.

For the Pesto: In a food processor, blend nuts and sage, slowly adding olive oil until all is incorporated. Season with pepper.

Yields approximately 3/4 cup.

For the Lamb: Ask your butcher for half of a leg of lamb, as fat- and sinew-free as possible.

Preheat the oven to 375°F. On the inside of the lamb, make 4 or 5 cuts, flattening out the meat. Rub lamb heavily with pesto inside and out. Roll and tie tightly with butcher's twine. In a hot pan, sear the outside of the lamb. Transfer to an oven pan and roast for 15 to 20 minutes, or until internal temperature reaches 115 to 120°F for medium-rare.

To Serve: At the top of each individual serving plate, spoon about 1/3 cup Bean Mash. Place 1/4 of the Braised Vegetables across the bottom of the plate, then top with 4 or 5 small slices of the lamb. Ladle about 1/4 cup of the Lamb Demi-Glace over the meat. Garnish with the chopped sage.

ROSEMARY PORK LOIN WITH BAKED APPLE

ROSEMARY PORK LOIN WITH BAKED APPLE

Serves 4

For the Pork Loin:
2 POUNDS PORK LOIN
1 TABLESPOON OLIVE OIL
1 TEASPOON SALT
1 TEASPOON BLACK PEPPER
6 SPRIGS ROSEMARY

For the Baked Apples:
3/4 CUP BUTTER
1/2 CUP BROWN SUGAR
1 CINNAMON STICK
2 TABLESPOONS OLIVE OIL
2 GREEN APPLES, PEELED, CORED AND
   CUT IN HALF
1/4 CUP CHICKEN STOCK*
1/2 TEASPOON SALT
10 BLACK PEPPERCORNS

For the Pork Jus:
1/4 CUP OLIVE OIL
1/2 POUND PORK SCRAPS
2 LARGE SHALLOTS, CHOPPED
PEEL AND CORE FROM 2 GREEN APPLES
1 TEASPOON BLACK PEPPERCORNS
1 BAY LEAF
3 CUPS CHICKEN STOCK*
1/4 CUP PAN DRIPPINGS FROM BAKED APPLES
1 TEASPOON SALT

*See Appendix

For the Beans:
2 TABLESPOONS OLIVE OIL
1/4 CUP ROAST SHALLOTS*, PEELED
   AND SLICED
1 CUP YELLOW WAX BEANS, TRIMMED
1 CUP GREEN BEANS, TRIMMED

For the Tuscan Bread Crumbs:
1/4 CUP BUTTER
1/2 CUP BREAD CRUMBS
1/2 TEASPOON GARLIC, MINCED
1 TEASPOON PARSLEY, CHOPPED
1 TEASPOON OREGANO, CHOPPED
SALT AND PEPPER TO TASTE

*Chef's note:
If you purchase a
pork loin that is
pre-trimmed, ask
the butcher for a
1/2 pound of pork
scraps for the
Pork Jus.*

For the Pork Loin: Preheat oven to
375°F. Rub the pork with olive oil; sprinkle with salt
and pepper. Tie the pork with 6 loops of butcher's
twine, tucking the rosemary under the twine. On a
cooktop, sear the pork in a hot pan, then transfer to a
roasting pan. Roast in the oven for 35 to 45 minutes,
or until internal temperature of 130°F is reached. Let
rest 5 minutes before slicing.

For the Baked Apples: Preheat oven to 375°F. In a saucepan, heat butter and sugar, mixing until blended. Add cinnamon stick and reserve. In a hot, oven-proof sauté pan, heat olive oil on the cook-top and lightly brown the apple slices. Add the Chicken Stock to the apples, cooking for 2 minutes. Add the butter and sugar mixture; season with the salt and peppercorns. Bake for 10 to 15 minutes, or until apples are tender and golden brown. Reserve Baked Apple pan drippings for Pork Jus.

Yields 4 baked apples halves.

For the Pork Jus: In a large saucepan, heat olive oil and cook the pork scraps for 15 minutes, stirring occasionally. Drain. Add the shallots, apple peels and cores, peppercorns and bay leaf, cooking for 5 more minutes. Add the Chicken Stock* and reduce to 1/2 volume. Strain. Stir in Baked Apple drippings and salt.

Yields approximately 1 3/4 cups.

For the Beans: In a sauté pan, heat the olive oil and sauté the shallots until caramelized. Add the beans and sauté for 3 to 4 minutes.

Yields 2 cups beans.

For the Tuscan Bread Crumbs: Brown the butter in a sauté pan, then add the bread crumbs, herbs and seasonings. Sauté until all is incorporated.

Yields approximately 1/2 cup.

To Serve: Place 4 slices Pork Loin and 1 Baked Apple half, sliced into thirds, on each in-dividual serving plate, topping with 1/4 cup Pork Jus. Place 1/2 cup Beans on each plate, then top with 2 tablespoons Tuscan Bread Crumbs.

SEA BASS WITH BRAISED FENNEL
AND SHALLOTS
Serves 4

For the Braised Fennel:
1/4 CUP OLIVE OIL
3 SHALLOTS, ROUGHLY CHOPPED
3 FENNEL BULBS
1 TEASPOON SALT
1 TEASPOON BLACK PEPPERCORNS
1 TEASPOON FENNEL SEEDS
1 BAY LEAF
1 QUART CHICKEN STOCK*

For the Braised Shallots:
1 TABLESPOON OLIVE OIL
8 WHOLE, LARGE SHALLOTS, PEELED
1/2 TEASPOON SALT
1/2 TEASPOON BLACK PEPPER
1 TEASPOON PARSLEY, CHOPPED
1/2 CUP CHICKEN STOCK*

For the Saffron Broth:
1/4 CUP OLIVE OIL
1 CARROT, CUT INTO LARGE PIECES
2 LEEKS, WHITE PART ONLY, CUT INTO QUARTERS
2 RIBS CELERY, CUT INTO LARGE PIECES
1 LARGE ONION, CUT INTO CHUNKS
PINCH SAFFRON THREADS
1 TEASPOON WHITE PEPPERCORNS
2 TABLESPOONS SALT
3 PARSLEY SPRIGS
2 BAY LEAVES
6 THYME SPRIGS

*See Appendix

2 POUNDS SEA BASS OR WHITE
 FISH BONES
1 CUP CHARDONNAY
1 1/2 QUARTS WATER

For the Sea Bass:
4 PIECES CHILEAN SEA BASS
OLIVE OIL
SALT AND PEPPER TO TASTE

FOR THE GARNISH:
FENNEL THREADS

Chef's note: When you're cooking the Braised Fennel, use a fork to test for doneness. If the fork is easily inserted and the fennel slides off the fork it's done. A purchased fish broth, "doctored" with saffron threads, can be substituted for the Saffron Broth.

For the Braised Fennel:
Preheat oven to 375°F. Heat a 3-quart saucepan, then add olive oil, shallots and fennel bulbs. Lightly brown on all sides. Add the salt, peppercorns, fennel seeds and bay leaf, continuing to brown. When the fennel bulbs are well seared, add Chicken Stock, then transfer to an oven-proof pan. Cover with aluminum foil, place in oven and braise until tender, approximately 20 to 30 minutes. Cut half the bulbs into small wedges; julienne the rest.
Yields 3 fennel bulbs.

For the Braised Shallots: Heat a sauté pan, add olive oil and whole shallots, sautéing until the shallots are lightly caramelized. Add the salt, pepper and parsley, sautéing for 30 more seconds. Add the Chicken Stock, reduce heat to low and simmer until shallots are transparent. Let shallots cool in liquid. Slice thickly. *Yields 8 shallots.*

For the Saffron Broth: In a large stock pot, heat the olive oil. Add the vegetables, seasonings and herbs, sautéing for 3 to 4 minutes. Add sea bass bones, Chardonnay and water. Simmer for 4 hours. Strain through a fine metal sieve lined with cheesecloth. Return broth to pot, heat and reduce by half. Adjust seasonings. *Yields approximately 1 quart.*

For the Sea Bass: Preheat oven to 350°F. Brush the sea bass with olive oil; season with salt and pepper. In a hot, oven-proof sauté pan, heat more olive oil and sear sea bass on one side. Turn the fish and put the pan in the oven for 3 to 5 minutes.

To Serve: On each individual serving plate, place 1/4 of the julienned Braised Fennel and 1/4 of the sliced Braised Shallots in the center of the plate. Top with the Sea Bass, then place quartered Braised Fennel around the fish. Ladle 1/4 cup Saffron Broth around the plate. Garnish with chopped fennel threads.

BROILED PRAWNS WITH GRIDDLED POTATO RISOTTO

BROILED PRAWNS WITH
GRIDDLED POTATO RISOTTO
Serves 4

For the Griddled Potato Risotto:
2 TABLESPOONS OLIVE OIL
2 LEEKS, WHITE PART ONLY, DICED
1 TABLESPOON GARLIC, CHOPPED
1 TABLESPOON SHALLOTS, CHOPPED
4 LARGE RUSSET POTATOES, PEELED AND DICED
2 1/4 CUPS CHICKEN STOCK*
3/4 CUP HEAVY CREAM
2 TABLESPOONS BUTTER
1 CUP PARMESAN CHEESE, GRATED
1 TABLESPOON SALT
2 TEASPOONS BLACK PEPPER
2 TABLESPOONS PARSLEY, CHOPPED
OLIVE OIL FOR GRIDDLING

For the Shrimp Beurre Blanc:
1 TABLESPOON OLIVE OIL
1 TABLESPOON SHALLOTS, CHOPPED
1 CUP SHRIMP STOCK*
1/4 CUP COLD UNSALTED BUTTER, CUT INTO
   CUBES
1 TEASPOON SALT
1/2 TEASPOON BLACK PEPPER
1 TEASPOON PARSLEY, CHOPPED

For the Fried Leek Garnish:
1/2 CUP LEEK BOTTOMS, JULIENNED
1/4 CUP CORNSTARCH
PINCH SALT
PINCH BLACK PEPPER
2 CUPS CANOLA OIL FOR FRYING

For the Broiled Prawns:
12 LARGE PRAWNS, SHELLS ON
1 LARGE ZUCCHINI, QUARTERED LENGTHWISE
OLIVE OIL
SALT AND PEPPER TO TASTE

FOR THE GARNISH:
2 TABLESPOONS CHIVES, CHOPPED

*See Appendix

For the Griddled Potato Risotto: In a sauté pan, heat olive oil and sauté half the leeks, and all of the garlic and shallots for 1 minute or until translucent. Add the potatoes and sauté for 2 minutes. Add the Chicken Stock 1/2 cup at a time, cooking until almost evaporated. Add the cream, reducing by 2/3 volume. Stir in all of the butter and the Parmesan. Season with salt, pepper and parsley. Stir in the rest of the leeks. Pour into a shallow pan to cool. Spoon about 1/2 cup of the potato mixture onto a hot, oiled griddle, repeating until the mixture is gone. Griddle until crispy on both sides. *Yields 8 cakes.*

For the Shrimp Beurre Blanc: In a hot sauté pan, heat the olive oil and sauté the shallots for 2 minutes over low heat. Add the Shrimp Stock, reducing to 1/4 of its volume. Whisk in the cold butter. Add salt, pepper and parsley. Reserve warm.

Yields 1/2 cup.

For the Fried Leek Garnish: Wash and dry the julienned leeks. Mix together the cornstarch, salt and pepper. Toss the leeks in the cornstarch mixture, coating evenly. Set the coated leeks aside for 15 minutes to absorb the cornstarch. Heat the oil in a deep frying pan or wok and fry the leeks for about 3 minutes or until they are crispy and golden.

Drain on paper towels.

For the Broiled Prawns: Coat the prawns and zucchini with olive oil; season with salt and pepper. Grill for about 6 or 7 minutes, or until the prawns are medium-rare and the zucchini is the desired doneness. Cut each zucchini quarter into 4 pieces.

To Serve: Place 2 Potato Risotto cakes in the center of each individual serving plate. Fan three Prawns on each plate with the tails resting on the cakes. Place 4 pieces of zucchini between the Prawns. Top each serving with about 2 tablespoons Shrimp Beurre Blanc. Garnish with the Fried Leeks and chopped chives.

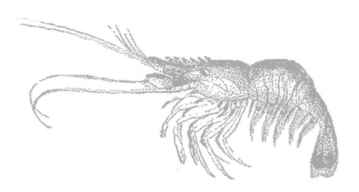

good night

Serenely full, the epicure would say, Fate cannot harm me,

I have dined today.

~Anonymous

APPLE TART WITH VANILLA ICE CREAM

Serves 6

For the Crust:

1 1/4 CUPS ALL-PURPOSE FLOUR
1/2 CUP SUGAR
1/2 CUP WALNUTS, CHOPPED
1 3/4 TEASPOONS BAKING POWDER
1/2 TEASPOON SALT
1/4 CUP UNSALTED BUTTER
2 EGGS

For the Smear Sauce:

1 CUP BROWN SUGAR
1/2 CUP BUTTER
1/4 CUP HONEY
2 TABLESPOONS WATER

For the Filling:

3 QUARTS WATER
JUICE OF 2 LEMONS
1 CUP SUGAR
9 GRANNY SMITH APPLES, PEELED,
  CORED AND THICKLY SLICED

TO SERVE:

GRANULATED SUGAR FOR TOPPING
6 SCOOPS VANILLA ICE CREAM
POWDERED SUGAR

Chef's note: This rustic, northern Italian apple tart should be served warm so that the ice cream melts through the edges of the apples and down the sides of the crust to form a vanilla sauce.

For the Crust: Preheat oven to 375°F. Using an electric mixer, blend all ingredients, adding eggs last. Divide dough into 6 equal parts. Spray six 6-inch springform pans with vegetable oil baking spray. Pat dough into the pans to a thickness of 1/4-inch or less. Bake for 6 to 8 minutes or until golden brown. *Yields 6 crusts.*

For the Smear Sauce: Using an electric mixer, mix all ingredients until butter is completely incorporated. Refrigerate until ready to use. *Yields 1 3/4 cups sauce.*

For the Filling: In a large saucepan, combine water, lemon juice and sugar. Bring to a simmer. Add apple slices and poach for 5 minutes. Using a slotted spoon, remove apple slices from water; drain on paper towels.

To Serve: Preheat oven to 375°F. Spread 3 tablespoons Smear Sauce onto the bottom of each baked crust. Divide apple mixture into 6 parts and layer into each crust. Bake for 5 minutes. Remove tarts from oven, open springform pans and cool. Sprinkle each tart with sugar. Place under broiler until sugar is caramelized. Top each tart with a scoop of vanilla ice cream. Dust with powdered sugar.

BREAD PUDDING WITH AMARETTO SAUCE

Serves 6

For the Bread Pudding: Preheat oven to 250°F. In a saucepan, bring milk to a boil. Add semolina and whisk constantly until the mixture thickens to a cream consistency. Remove from heat and whip milk mixture with an electric mixer on low speed for 1 minute. Add eggs, condensed milk and vanilla extract. Reserve mixture. Put 1 1/2 cups of bread cubes and 1/2 cup of mangoes into each of 6 individual (16-ounce) soufflé dishes. Cover with 1/2 cup of the milk mixture. Set bowls in a deep baking dish, filled with water to within 3/4-inch of the top of the baking bowls. Bake for 45 minutes or until Bread Pudding is slightly firm to the touch. Cool for 30 minutes before serving.

For the Amaretto Sauce: In a saucepan, heat milk and cream to a boil. Remove from heat and reserve. In a mixing bowl, blend eggs and sugar together, but do not whip. Pour egg mixture into a separate saucepan. Gradually pour hot milk mixture into egg mixture over low heat, bringing to a simmer. Pour into a clean bowl; chill over ice. Stir in vanilla and Amaretto.

To Serve: Offer the Amaretto Sauce "on the side" so that guests can add a little at a time to their Bread Pudding.

For the Bread Pudding:
4 CUPS MILK
1/4 CUP SEMOLINA FLOUR
2 EGGS
4 CUPS CONDENSED MILK
1 TABLESPOON VANILLA EXTRACT
9 CUPS WHITE BREAD, CUBED
3 CUPS MANGOES, PEELED AND CUBED

For the Amaretto Sauce:
3/4 CUP MILK
3/4 CUP HEAVY CREAM
4 EGGS
1/2 CUP SUGAR
1 1/2 TEASPOONS VANILLA EXTRACT
2 TABLESPOONS AMARETTO

*Chef's note:
We like to lighten this comforting, peasant-style dessert with a touch of mango.*

LEMON TART WITH STRAWBERRY SAUCE AND FRUIT RELISH

Serves 12

For the Lemon Tart Crust:

1 1/2 CUPS UNSALTED BUTTER

3/4 CUP SUGAR

3 EGGS

1 1/2 CUPS ALL-PURPOSE FLOUR

3/4 CUP UNSALTED PISTACHIO NUTS, FINELY GROUND

PINCH OF SALT

For the Lemon Cream Filling:

3 WHOLE EGGS

3 EGG YOLKS

1/4 CUP SUGAR

JUICE OF 4 LEMONS

1 TABLESPOON LEMON ZEST

1 CUP UNSALTED BUTTER, CUT INTO SMALL PIECES

SUGAR FOR CARAMELIZING

For the Strawberry Sauce:

2 CUPS STRAWBERRIES, FRESH OR FROZEN

1/4 CUP SUGAR

1 TABLESPOON CORNSTARCH

1/4 CUP WATER

For the Fruit Relish:

3/4 CUP STRAWBERRIES, DICED

3/4 CUP ORANGE SEGMENTS, DICED

1 TABLESPOON MINT, CHOPPED

1 TABLESPOON SUGAR

For the Rolled Florentine Cookies:

1 CUP UNSALTED PISTACHIOS, FINELY GROUND

3/4 CUP BUTTER

3/4 CUP SUGAR

3/4 CUP CAKE FLOUR

1/2 CUP LIGHT CORN SYRUP

1 TEASPOON VANILLA EXTRACT

1 TEASPOON SALT

For the Crust: Preheat oven to 350°F. Cream butter and sugar until fluffy. Add eggs 1 at a time until blended. Add flour, pistachios and salt, blending until just mixed. Roll dough to a 12-inch round and transfer into an ungreased 11-inch tart pan with a removable bottom. Bake for 20 minutes, or until the crust is golden brown.

For the Filling: Fill the bottom of a double boiler 3/4 full of water. Over the boiling water, combine the eggs, egg yolks, sugar, lemon juice and zest, whisking continuously until mixture thickens. Remove from heat and add butter, stirring until the butter melts. Pour filling into the baked crust, let cool, then freeze for 4 hours. Heavily sprinkle sugar over the top of the tart, then place under the broiler until the top is golden brown.

For the Strawberry Sauce: Heat strawberries and sugar in a saucepan until boiling. Pour mixture through a strainer into a clean saucepan, return to heat and bring to a boil. Add cornstarch and water, whisking for about 2 minutes. Remove from heat and refrigerate. *Yields 3/4 cup.*

For the Relish: Toss together ingredients lightly and refrigerate. *Yields 1 1/2 cups.*

For the Cookies: Preheat oven to 375°F. Using an electric mixer, blend all ingredients. Line a baking sheet with parchment paper that has been sprayed with a vegetable oil baking spray. Using a spatula, spread the dough into 2-by-4-inch rectangles on the baking sheet and bake for about 20 minutes or until golden brown. Remove from oven. While the cookies are still warm, start with their long sides and roll them into a tube shape over a thin dowel or pencil. If the cookie becomes too firm before the rolling is complete, return to oven to soften. Let cool into desired shape.

Yields 12 cookies.

To Serve: Cut Lemon Tart into 12 pieces. Place 1 slice on each serving dish, topped with 2 tablespoons Strawberry Sauce and 2 tablespoons Fruit Relish. Place 1 Rolled Florentine Cookie to the side of the tart slice.

Chef's note: Any fruit may be substituted for the Fruit Relish, which, served alone, is a great, light dessert for a warm climate.

FLOURLESS CHOCOLATE CAKE WITH HAZELNUT ICE CREAM

Serves 8

For the Cake:

10 OUNCES SEMI-SWEET CHOCOLATE

3/4 CUP BUTTER

5 EGGS, SEPARATED

2 TEASPOONS COFFEE EXTRACT OR 1/2 CUP
    ESPRESSO

1 TEASPOON LEMON JUICE

2 TABLESPOONS SUGAR

For the Almond Lace Cookies:

1/2 CUP BUTTER

3/4 CUP SUGAR

1 TEASPOON VANILLA EXTRACT

1/2 TEASPOON SALT

1/2 CUP LIGHT CORN SYRUP

3/4 CUP CAKE FLOUR

3/4 CUP ALMONDS, FINELY CHOPPED

TO SERVE:

2 CUPS CHOCOLATE SAUCE*

1 QUART HAZELNUT ICE CREAM

1 PINT FRESH RASPBERRIES

1/4 CUP HAZELNUTS, CHOPPED

*See Appendix

Chef's note:
This is by far the richest, most decadent dessert on our menu—and a personal favorite. You can serve any flavor ice cream and top with the berries of your choice.

For the Cake: Preheat oven to 325°F. Melt together the chocolate and butter over a double boiler or in the microwave, stirring well. Remove from heat. In a separate bowl, whip the egg yolks and coffee until fluffy. Fold chocolate mixture into egg yolks; reserve.

With an electric mixer, whip egg whites at high speed to form soft peaks. Add lemon juice and continue whipping. Add sugar when the egg whites are fluffy and firm. Fold the egg whites into the chocolate mixture, mixing just enough to blend. Spray 8 small savarin ring molds with vegetable oil baking spray. Fill each mold to just below the rim with the cake mixture. Bake for 20 minutes. *Yields 8 cakes.*

For the Almond Lace Cookies: Preheat the oven to 375°F. Using an electric mixer, cream together butter and sugar. Add vanilla and salt, mixing well, then gradually add the corn syrup and flour. Fold in the almonds. Line a baking sheet with parchment paper that has been sprayed with vegetable oil baking spray. Spread the cookie dough on the pan approximately 1/4-inch thick. Bake for 20 minutes, or until golden brown. Remove from oven. While still warm, score the sheet of cookies into 12 triangles, approximately 1 1/2 inches in size. Cool and remove from tray. *Yields 12 cookies.*

To Serve: For each serving, place a still-warm Flourless Chocolate Cake in the center of a plate. Pour 1/4 cup Chocolate Sauce around the edge of the cake so it spills onto the plate. Place a scoop of ice cream in the center of the cake; top with an Almond Lace Cookie. Sprinkle with raspberries and hazelnuts.

PROFITEROLES WITH NEAPOLITAN ICE CREAM

Serves 6

For the Profiteroles: Preheat the oven to 400°F. In a saucepan, bring the milk and butter to a boil. Add the flour and salt, stirring with a wooden spoon. Cook for 1 or 2 minutes. Transfer mixture to a bowl, and, using an electric mixer, add eggs slowly. Line a baking sheet with parchment paper. Using a medium-size pastry bag with a #5 or #6 round tip, pipe dough into quarter-size rounds, 1/4-inch thick. Bake at 400°F for 5 minutes, then lower temperature to 375°F. Continue baking until pastry is firm and golden brown. Remove from oven and cool. *Yields 18 to 21 pastries.*

For the Caramel Sauce: In a saucepan, boil water together with sugar and lemon juice, making sure there is no sugar residue on the edge of the pan. (To remove sugar residue, brush the edge with a water-dampened pastry brush.) When the sugar mixture reaches a golden color, add the butter and cream, mixing thoroughly. Remove from heat and cool. *Yields 2 cups.*

To Serve: Slice the Profiteroles in half horizontally, hollowing out a bit of the bottom half. Place 1 ice cream scoop into the bottom half of the Profiterole, and top with the other half. On each individual serving plate, place 3 filled Profiteroles, dust with powdered sugar and alternately drizzle with Caramel and Chocolate sauces to form a striped pattern.

For the Profiteroles:
1 CUP MILK
1/4 POUND UNSALTED BUTTER
1 1/3 CUPS ALL-PURPOSE FLOUR
1/2 TEASPOON SALT
6 EGGS

For the Caramel Sauce:
1 CUP WATER
2 CUPS SUGAR
1 TEASPOON LEMON JUICE
1/4 POUND BUTTER
1/4 CUP HEAVY CREAM

TO SERVE:
18 SMALL SCOOPS NEAPOLITAN ICE CREAM
POWDERED SUGAR
1 1/2 CUPS CHOCOLATE SAUCE*

*See Appendix

Chef's note: Profiteroles are a classic French pastry that can be filled with custards, whipped cream or ice cream. The dough is called pâte 'a choux. Our favorite way of serving this is with Neapolitan ice cream.

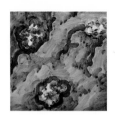

appendix

CHOCOLATE SAUCE
Yields 2 Cups

In a heavy saucepan, heat cream to a near boil. In a glass bowl, break chocolate into chunks. Pour the cream over the chocolate and stir with a spatula until smooth. Let cool at room temperature.

1/2 CUP HEAVY CREAM
16 OUNCES SEMI-SWEET CHOCOLATE

CHIANTI VINAIGRETTE
Yields Approximately 1 Quart

In a heavy-bottomed pot, heat and reduce the Chianti to 1/4 of its volume. Pour into a mixing bowl; whisk in Chicken Stock and vinegar. Add the sugar, garlic, shallots, herbs, salt, pepper and Gorgonzola. Let steep for 30 minutes. Slowly whisk in the olive oil.

1 QUART CHIANTI
1/4 CUP CHICKEN STOCK (SEE PAGE 90)
1/2 CUP RED WINE VINEGAR
1 TABLESPOON SUGAR
1 TABLESPOON GARLIC, CHOPPED
1 TABLESPOON SHALLOTS, CHOPPED
1 TABLESPOON PARSLEY, CHOPPED
1 TABLESPOON ROSEMARY, CHOPPED
1 TABLESPOON SAGE, CHOPPED
1 TABLESPOON CHIVES, CHOPPED
2 TEASPOONS SALT
1 TEASPOON BLACK PEPPER
2 TABLESPOONS GORGONZOLA CHEESE, GRATED
1 3/4 CUPS OLIVE OIL

BALSAMIC VINAIGRETTE
Yields 1 1/4 Cups

1 TABLESPOON DIJON MUSTARD
1 TABLESPOON LEMON JUICE
1 TABLESPOON GARLIC, CHOPPED
2 TABLESPOONS SHALLOTS, CHOPPED
1 TABLESPOON CHIVES, CHOPPED
1/4 CUP BALSAMIC VINEGAR
3/4 CUP OLIVE OIL
1 TEASPOON SALT
1/2 TEASPOON BLACK PEPPER

In a mixing bowl, whisk together mustard, lemon juice, garlic, shallots, chives and the vinegar. Add oil slowly, while whisking rapidly to form an emulsion. Add salt and pepper.

FOCACCIA BREAD
Yields 6 8-Inch Rounds or 1 Large Sheet

For the Topping:
1/2 CUP OLIVE OIL
1/3 CUP ROSEMARY
1/3 CUP GARLIC, CHOPPED
1/3 CUP PARMESAN CHEESE, GRATED

For the Bread:
2 PACKAGES (2 TABLESPOONS) DRY YEAST
2 1/2 CUPS WARM WATER
6 CUPS ALL-PURPOSE FLOUR
3/4 TABLESPOON SALT
1 TABLESPOON SUGAR
2 TABLESPOONS OLIVE OIL

For the Topping: Mix together all of the ingredients.

For the Bread: Preheat oven to 400°F. Dissolve yeast in water. Using a mixer with a dough attachment, blend flour, salt, sugar, oil and yeast liquid, mixing on low speed for 8 minutes. On a floured surface, divide dough into 6 equal rounds. Place rounds on a sheet pan or pans coated with olive oil. Let dough rest for 10 minutes. Stretch dough into 8-inch rounds. Brush Topping onto each round. Bake for approximately 15 minutes, or until the rounds are golden brown.

POMMES FRITES
Serves 4

Wash the potatoes, then julienne. Soak the potatoes in warm water until ready to fry. Heat the oil in a wok. Fry potatoes until crispy and golden brown. Drain. In a large mixing bowl, toss hot potatoes with salt, pepper and parsley. Serve immediately.

3 LARGE RUSSET POTATOES, UNPEELED
3-4 CUPS VEGETABLE OIL
2 PINCHES SALT
1 PINCH BLACK PEPPER
1 TABLESPOON PARSLEY, FINELY CHOPPED

GRILLED MUSHROOMS
Yields 4 Mushrooms

Combine the vinegar, olive oil, garlic, rosemary, salt and pepper. Remove stems and lungs from mushrooms; marinate in the vinegar mixture for 1 hour. Grill until tender, then remove from heat and let cool in a pan with a tight cover.

2 TABLESPOONS BALSAMIC VINEGAR
1/4 CUP OLIVE OIL
1 TEASPOON GARLIC, CHOPPED
1 TEASPOON ROSEMARY, CHOPPED
1 TEASPOON SALT
1 TEASPOON BLACK PEPPER
4 LARGE PORTOBELLO MUSHROOMS

Chef's note: By cooling the Grilled Mushrooms in a tightly covered pan, you create a natural steaming that seals in their juices and flavor.

MUSHROOM STOCK
Yields Approximately 1 Gallon

Sauté the mushrooms, onions, carrot and garlic in the olive oil for about 10 minutes, or until the vegetables begin to caramelize. Add the peppercorns, herbs and chicken stock. Bring to a boil, then simmer approximately 40 to 45 minutes, or until reduced by half. Strain. Whisk the butter into the stock. Add salt.

3 POUNDS MUSHROOMS, STEMS AND CAPS, CHOPPED
1 LARGE CARROT, CUT INTO 2-INCH SLICES
2 LARGE ONIONS, CUT INTO CHUNKS
1 GARLIC CLOVE, CHOPPED
2 TABLESPOONS OLIVE OIL
1 TEASPOON BLACK PEPPERCORNS
1/2 BUNCH PARSLEY, CHOPPED
1/2 BUNCH SAGE, CHOPPED
1 1/2 GALLONS CHICKEN STOCK*
2 POUNDS BUTTER, CUT INTO PATTIES
1 TEASPOON SALT

Chef's note: This intense, buttery stock is also a good way to utilize leftover mushroom stems.

ROAST SHALLOTS
Yields 16 Shallots

16 LARGE SHALLOTS, UNPEELED
OLIVE OIL
SALT AND PEPPER TO TASTE

Preheat oven to 375°F. Coat the unpeeled shallots with olive oil; season with salt and pepper. Wrap shallots in aluminum foil; place on baking sheet and roast for 40 minutes or until tender. Peel outer skin before serving.

ROAST GARLIC
Yields 2 Tablespoons Purée

1 LARGE GARLIC BULB, UNPEELED
OLIVE OIL
SALT AND PEPPER TO TASTE

Preheat oven to 325°F. Slice the top off the unpeeled garlic bulb. Coat with olive oil; season with salt and pepper. Wrap garlic in aluminum foil, place on a baking sheet and roast for about 20 minutes or until the bulb is soft. Let cool, then squeeze the bulb to extract the purée.

SHRIMP STOCK
Yields Approximately 1 1/2 Quarts

1/4 CUP OLIVE OIL
3 LARGE CARROTS, CUT INTO 2-INCH SLICES
6 CELERY RIBS, CUT INTO 2-INCH SLICES
2 LARGE ONIONS, CUT INTO CHUNKS
6 ROMA (ITALIAN PLUM) TOMATOES, CHOPPED
1 WHOLE GARLIC BULB, UNPEELED, CUT IN HALF
1/4 CUP TOMATO PASTE
2 POUNDS SHRIMP SHELLS
1 POUND LOBSTER BODIES (NO CLAWS, NO TAILS)
2 BAY LEAVES
1 BUNCH THYME SPRIGS
1 TEASPOON BLACK PEPPERCORNS
1 CUP CHARDONNAY

Heat the olive oil in a large stock pot. Add the vegetables and garlic bulb and sauté for 4 to 5 minutes. Add the tomato paste, shrimp shells, lobster bodies, herbs and peppercorns. Cook for 3 to 5 minutes, stirring continuously. Add the Chardonnay, cooking for 5 more minutes. Add 1 gallon of water, bring to a boil, then reduce heat, simmering for 4 hours. Strain the stock through a fine sieve lined with cheesecloth. Reduce the stock by half.

BEEF OR LAMB DEMI-GLACE
Yields Approximately 2 Cups

Heat a large stock pot, add olive oil and beef scraps and brown thoroughly. Add onion, celery, garlic, carrots, tomatoes and parsley and continue browning for 10 minutes. Add tomato paste and continue browning until beef is cooked and vegetables are caramelized, about 2 minutes. Add the Chianti and the peppercorns. Reduce the Chianti to 1/4 of its volume. Add water, salt and bay leaf, simmering over medium heat for 2 hours. Strain, then reduce over medium heat to 1/2 of its volume. Adjust seasonings and sprinkle with parsley.

To make a Lamb Demi-Glace, substitute lamb for beef scraps and Cabernet Sauvignon for the Chianti.

1/4 CUP OLIVE OIL
2 POUNDS BEEF SCRAPS
1 LARGE ONION, CHOPPED
2 RIBS CELERY, CHOPPED
1 CLOVE GARLIC, CHOPPED
1 LARGE CARROT, CHOPPED
1/2 CUP TOMATOES, CHOPPED
1 TABLESPOON PARSLEY, CHOPPED
1 TABLESPOON TOMATO PASTE
1 CUP CHIANTI
1 TEASPOON BLACK PEPPERCORNS
1 QUART WATER
1/4 TEASPOON SALT
1 BAY LEAF
CHOPPED PARSLEY

Chef's note: When you add the Chianti to the browned meat and vegetables, it becomes a deglazing process, lifting the sugars from the sides of the pot.

ROAST CHICKEN
Serves 2

Preheat the oven to 375°F. Stuff the cleaned chicken with the chopped lemons and bay leaves. Rub the outside with the olive tapenade. Mix together dry ingredients; sprinkle over chicken. Roast for 45 minutes or until the skin is golden brown and the juices run clear. Reserve the pan drippings.

1 3 1/2-POUND ROASTING CHICKEN
2 LEMONS, CUT INTO CHUNKS
3 BAY LEAVES
1/4 CUP OLIVE TAPENADE, PURCHASED
1 TEASPOON PAPRIKA
1/2 TEASPOON GROUND OREGANO
1 TEASPOON GRANULATED GARLIC
2 TEASPOONS KOSHER SALT
1 TEASPOON BLACK PEPPER

Chef's note: A purchased seasoning salt can be substituted for the dry ingredients.

CHICKEN STOCK
Yields Approximately 1/2 Gallon

5 POUNDS CHICKEN BONES, NECKS AND WINGS
1/4 CUP OLIVE OIL
2 ONIONS, CUT INTO LARGE CHUNKS
2 CARROTS, CUT INTO 2-INCH SLICES
2 LEEKS, CUT INTO 2-INCH SLICES
4 CELERY RIBS, CUT INTO
   2-INCH SLICES
2 GARLIC CLOVES, CUT IN HALF
2 CUPS CHARDONNAY
1 TABLESPOON BLACK
   PEPPERCORNS
4 BAY LEAVES
1/2 BUNCH PARSLEY
3 QUARTS WATER

Chef's note:

In our restaurant kitchen, we make a "remouillage," or a second cooking of our basic Chicken Stock. We add enough water to again cover the drained chicken and vegetables by 2 inches, bring to a boil, then simmer for 6 more hours. This is then strained and used as a richer stock. You can also reduce this by half and add herbs to create a light sauce. Naturally, if you don't have the time or inclination to make your own chicken stock, purchased stock can be substituted.

Rinse chicken bones and parts; reserve. In a large stock pot, heat olive oil and sauté onions, carrots, leeks, celery and garlic for 5 to 7 minutes. Add Chardonnay and cook for about 5 more minutes, until vegetables become transparent. Add chicken bones and parts, peppercorns, bay leaves and parsley, cooking for an additional 5 to 7 minutes. Add water and bring to a boil, skimming foam and fat. Lower heat and simmer for 4 hours. Strain before using. This stock can be frozen.

To make a Brown Chicken Stock, preheat the oven to 375° F. Place the chicken bones and parts in a deep baking pan and brown for approximately 15 to 20 minutes. Add the vegetables, 1 tablespoon tomato paste and the Chardonnay to the pan and return to oven for another 15 to 20 minutes. Transfer the chicken and vegetables to a large stock pot and continue as with the standard Chicken Stock recipe.

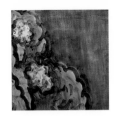

index

FROM LEFT TO RIGHT: Michael DeMaria, Perry Jermonte, David Judd, Michael Hoobler, Rick Watson

I LIVE ON TOASTED LIZARDS

PRICKLY PEARS, AND PARROT GIZZARDS

AND I'M REALLY FOND OF BEETLE PIE.

~CHARLES EDWARD CARRYE